AWAKEN YOUR
AUTHENTIC LEADERSHIP

AUTHENTIC LEADERSHIP CONVERSATIONS
FOR MEANINGFUL CONNECTION

"I first met Tana in the spring of 2017. Through her coaching she helped clarify my journey to become a Certified Organizational Coach. Her book *Awaken Your Authentic Leadership* resonated with me and validated my own approach to leading people. She encouraged me to challenge and reflect upon some of my beliefs and patterns, leading to new a fresh new approach to work and life for me.

In late 2017 I joined an organization that had become stuck. I wanted to approach this new role with my most authentic self and be fully present and never hesitate to do what was right and what I genuinely believed would make a difference. Focusing on values and purpose I set forth to make a significant impact as quickly as possible.

Leveraging my new knowledge and understanding, I immersed myself and evaluated what we needed to shift the existing culture to one of learning and growth. Once I had the buy in from the CEO to move forward, I engaged Tana and Laura to bring their Authentic Leadership Conversation training to our executive team, followed by team leaders and then the entire organization this year.

In early 2020 when the pandemic hit, we had to postpone our in person leadership training sessions and quickly pivoted to and created a new weekly company wide video meeting to create a safe space to share how we were feeling and make our company stronger in challenging and unprecedented times we find ourselves in.

I have no doubt that Tana's insight and dedicated practice of Authentic Leadership has positively impacted both our employee engagement and our double-digit revenue growth in the last two years."

Kerry Brock, MBA, Certified Organizational Coach, ACC

"Authentic Leadership Conversations™ are exactly that, authentic and conversations. They differ greatly from any "leadership workshop" I have either attended or facilitated; they are so much more. The theories and teachings surrounding topics such as "how to have difficult performance conversations" or "delegation" come to life in real time. There is an exchange of ideas, experiences, and opinions between all participants about the topic at hand which allows for practicing vulnerability, stepping out of one's comfort zone and leveling of the playing field by removing any leadership hierarchy for the duration of the conversation.

In addition to improving leadership skills, these conversations allow us to learn about each other. Assumptions are replaced with facts; journeys, mistakes and all, are shared; and the learning becomes lateral, between me as a facilitator, senior leaders, those just beginning their leadership journeys, and those somewhere in between."

Sarah Clarke, Coach, Authentic Leadership Program Facilitator

"I have been using the ALG topics for close to a decade now, both for my own development and with clients, in many sectors. What I know is that without a doubt, these materials inspire a deeper connection to self, leading to increased empathy and understanding of others. Overall, connection to self, connection to others."

Laura Mack, Executive and Leadership Coach,
Authentic Leadership Program Facilitator and Trainer

"I have been offering the Authentic Leadership Conversations™ for a few years now and my clients are enthusiastic about the impact these conversations are having in their life and leadership. These facilitated conversations are so unique and it's really about creating the conditions to get a bit uncomfortable. These conversations are unlike other conversations we normally have elsewhere. Things aren't tied up neatly and there isn't a set curriculum that we teach or learn. It's about finding our own meaning in the minimal structure provided. It's a privilege to know that when people leave our conversations, there are loose ends for each of us to examine, new scenarios to explore, and endless opportunities for self-reflection and action. And I am looking forward to having all of the action worksheets in one book to be able to look back on my own reflections and to see my growth as I embed more of these practices into my day to day leadership and life. As the host/facilitator, I also learn so much each time I have the opportunity to bring a new group together around these timely topics."

**Jenn Wicks, Executive and Leadership Coach,
Authentic Leadership Program Facilitator**

"To me, Authentic Leadership Conversations™ (ALCs) are about connection and communication — with oneself and with others. They encourage self-reflection and authentic communication to support personal and professional growth.

Both the content and the adaptability for the format make the conversations incredibly valuable for facilitators and participants. In either of those roles I have found "Saying No", "Navigating Transitions" and "Managing the Inner Critic" to be particularly powerful because they address questions that concern anyone, regardless of age, gender, profession or culture.

The diversity of audiences ALCs have been and still are being delivered to reflect that a leader really is "anyone who steps up and influences others". Personally, I have worked with expats, students and young professionals. Besides the adaptability of the material, ALCs can also be adapted as virtual format which I find incredibly valuable and important in the 21st century. I continue to be impressed how the nature of ALCs can create very strong connection among people who have never met in person. When I first met the group of facilitators that I had been having virtual conversations with in person, it felt like we had known each other personally for a long time.

Thanks to their great content, structure and adaptability ALCs are a high quality, customized program that I can offer my clients. ALCs invite participants to self-reflect and be vulnerable while also ensuring transfer of the new awareness into everyday life and work. Various clients have shared that they did not only enjoy the conversation itself but that their improved awareness changed the way they seem themselves and how interact with others both in their personal and professional life."

**Hannah Lambeck, Intercultural Trainer & Dialogue Facilitator,
Authentic Leadership Program Facilitator**

Other books by the Author

Awaken Your Authentic Leadership — Lead with Inner Clarity and Purpose

Awaken Your Authentic Leadership — Authenticity Journal

Coming Soon:

Awaken Your Authentic Leadership — Daring to Share Your Story: An Authentic Writing Guide by Tana Heminsley & Diana Reyers

Awaken Your Authentic Leadership — Parenting as a Leadership Journey by Tana Heminsley and Laura Mack

Tana Heminsley as a Contributing Author:

Daring to Share: 8 Brave Souls Sharing Their Authentic Road Trip — Volume 1 by Diana Reyers

Daring to Share: There to Here — 2nd Edition | Volume 1 by Diana Reyers

AWAKEN YOUR AUTHENTIC LEADERSHIP

Authentic Leadership Conversations for Meaningful Connection

TANA HEMINSLEY

AUTHENTIC LEADERSHIP GLOBAL
PUBLISHING DIVISION

Published by Authentic Leadership Global, 2020
ISBN: 978-1-7771921-2-9

Copyright © 2020 by Tana Heminsley

All rights reserved. This book or any portion thereof may not be reproduced or used in any manner whatsoever without the express written permission of the publisher except for the use of brief quotations in a book review.

Editor: Diana Reyers

Authentic Leadership Global, Inc. — Publishing Division
#2401-1005 Beach Avenue
Vancouver, B.C.
V6E 3W2
Canada

tana@leadauthentic.com
www.leadauthentic.com

For my Mom and Dad,
and my brothers Wes and Michael.

Thank you for all of the meaningful conversations over the years,
as well as your constant inspiration and support.

Table of Contents

Foreword by Diana Reyers 1

Introduction by Tana Heminsley 5

How to Use This Book 7

Overview of Topics 9

Understanding Authenticity and
Emotional Intelligence 13

Navigating Transitions 21

Managing the Inner Critic 29

Creating Work-Life Balance 41

Having Difficult Conversations 55

Saying No and Setting Boundaries 67

Integrating The Three Centers of Intelligence 77

Discovering New Models for Leadership 89

Having a Difficult Performance Conversation 97

Shifting Scarcity to Abundance Mindset 107

Leading and Living Congruent With Your Values 119

Managing Conflict 131

Learning to Delegate 145

Receiving and Giving Feedback 157

Cultivating Joy at Work 167

Building Relationships Authentically 173

Having Effective Meetings 183

Having Authentic Conversations 199

Bibliography 205

The History of Authentic Leadership Conversations™ 207

About the Author 209

As I get ready to publish this book, the world has changed. We are in the midst of a global pandemic where there are currently more than 2 million COVID-19 Coronavirus cases, 150,000 deaths, and 600,000 recovered.

It has only been 3.5 months since the initial signs of the outbreak, and during that time our lives, the lives of our families and friends, and the way we live have been forever altered.

Businesses, communities, provinces, states, countries, and global organizations are struggling to find the paths through this.

Our language now includes words like COVID-19, Coronavirus, pandemic, social distancing, self-isolation, N95 masks, contact tracing, and others.

The way we interact, while longing for connection, is based on lifesaving, physical distancing. Is this only for now or forever? No one knows.

The world, during and post COVID-19, is being re-imagined on a just-in-time basis. Changes to world views, policies and structures are essential. This pandemic is a wake-up call to old rules and ways of being that no longer serve us. There is a enormous challenge to find new ways of looking at the trade-offs where there are not only two options to the choice - failed economies and the loss of lives.

These conversations are essential. Aware and ethical individuals participating in them will make all the difference. Change will be strengthened by leaders who are able to be their best-selves and override unhelpful aspects of the mind and ego on a sometimes moment-to-moment basis.

The need for leaders with strong, moral, and ethical inner guidance systems is more important than ever. These are the authentic leaders.

Foreword by Diana Reyers

There is nothing more powerful than a meaningful conversation as it subconsciously moves us to a place of self-discovery and a deeper understanding of ourselves. Over the years, I found that we really can't live our truth unless we have that deep understanding of what our truth is as well as that of others. Without the clarity of knowing each other authentically, how can we be sure we are responding to what really is, rather than reacting to a perception of what we think we are experiencing? If we're unsure, we may wonder, *Is this the truth or is it just a story I've created in my head?*

When we have clarity about our truth, our values, beliefs, what we are passionate about and what motivates us, we actually feel when we are living in line with our reality; we experience an inner knowing from a place deep within our spirit. This innate energy provides us with an empowering connection to ourselves and provides us with the confidence to authentically connect with others.

However, when we are unclear about who we are, we become indecisive about how to show up in the world because we simply don't have the level of awareness we need to be the person we truly are, that part deep within us that is hibernating and waiting to be released. We end up showing up as the person we think others expect us to be and, although it doesn't feel right, it becomes our default because it's the only way we think we know. This creates the uncomfortable feeling of personal disconnection and dominos into the inability to connect with others. Eventually, the disconnection we are experiencing manifests into a build-up of inner stress or dis-ease, and often over time, presents as chronic emotional and physical illness.

I experienced this discomfort most of my life as I reacted to the people and world around me in a way I thought was expected instead of how my soul begged me to respond to it. I longed for connection and mistook this yearning as needing approval from others. Over time, this translated into me ignoring my authentic self and becoming a chameleon who presented characteristics and a way of being I believed others resonated with. I became very talented at being someone I was not and a person I interpreted others wanted me to be.

Putting on this façade became extremely prevalent within my career. I worked in organizations and with people who all did the same. Out of survival, the majority of the people I worked with developed personalities designed to please the leadership team who managed us. As much as we chose this way of being, it was because we felt a significant expectation to do, say, and be a certain way. If anyone tested the waters by suggesting something different, we were shamed and reprimanded, and if we were courageous enough to commit to our moral and ethical convictions, we were usually dismissed.

I quickly learned that my thoughts and emotions were not of value and that people-pleasing was. The message I received was that the world did not honour my individuality and I should not honour uniqueness in myself or others. My life felt like a big theatre production with all the actors reading lines from a script and none of the cast resonating with one minute of it. My mind became very chaotic and indecisive as I tried to fit into a society based on the deception that lacked the authentic way of being I craved. How the actors in this play of life reacted to one another lacked integrity all around.

At the age of forty-five, I became very ill from years of internal stress having manifested inside my physical body and presenting as an autoimmune disease. It now makes sense to me as I realize that I chose to not show my true self, so in order to cope emotionally, mentally and spiritually, I subconsciously defaulted to attacking my authenticity to keep her shunned and still. The slow deterioration of my soul manifested into physical debilitation and I had to leave a career, including a lucrative position. Seeking daily solace in a local coffee shop, I sat for hours reflecting on what was happening to me and I wondered why. Day after day, I sat by the fireplace in the café and grieved the loss of who I thought I was. I watched customers come and go and noticed that most seemed to be just going through the motions. I felt their deep disconnect with self and I didn't feel connected to any of them either; there was no joy emanating from them and I wondered when they too would be inflicted with illness.

After a few weeks, I snapped out of my hermitized state by following my need to feel connection. I began chatting with those sitting closest to me in that coffee shop. I experienced a sudden urge to share deep feelings and thoughts that percolated up within me. I believe that sitting in that café for weeks provided my mind and soul with the space it needed to bring who I really am to the surface and the need to meet anyone else's expectations began to dissipate. Because of this natural shift into a new mindset, I began sharing things about myself with complete vulnerability and to complete strangers. The result was that these very people who seemed to move like robots before suddenly sat up and listened to what I was sharing. It wasn't because I had something amazing to say, but that they felt the distinct difference between shallow chit chat and meaningful conversation. They too were yearning for the connection that comes with speaking and being our truth.

By having these transparent conversations with others, I began learning all kinds of things about myself. I discovered aspects about myself I felt all along but didn't have the awareness within the degree of personal evolution I had achieved to articulate what lay deep within me. I realized that I was drawn to the magical experience of conversation from a very early age because it provided me the beginning stages of feeling connected. I just always seemed to stop short of the next step within feeling fully connected because I didn't understand myself well enough to confidently move forward into the power of it. I needed to have the confidence to really get to know myself in order to be who I truly am while accepting any perceived trade-offs along the way. After doing the work, I eventually learned that I am not damaged, I'm just personally evolving and there is no consequence big enough that will keep me from sharing my true self with the world.

I met Tana Heminsley through a close and long-time friend of mine, Karen Heminsley, after explaining to her that I wanted to support others to be able to step into their power as their authentic selves just as I had through the positive impact of conversation. Because I shared this with Karen, she introduced me to her sister-in-law, Tana, and after meeting her and moving through her conversation programs, the way I responded to my life shifted as greatly as my perception to it did. I began truly seeing myself and sought seeing others as we really are from our soulful selves. Reality suddenly replaced the fantasy I had been hiding within.

Tana is an intuitive genius when it comes to guiding individuals towards their authenticity. The Conversation Series you are about to embark on will provide you with a step-by-step process towards inner clarity. Using it to support your own personal evolution will amaze and enlighten you while, taking what you learn to support those you work with or for, will forever change how you experience this thing we call *work*. I no longer describe work as something I do every day as a means to make a living; it is instead something that provides me with great purpose and is a conduit for me to express myself within it and be impactful as I inspire others to share their stories without shame or blame. I like to describe my value of work as *effectiveness*.

Since working with Tana, I have facilitated the Authentic Leadership Conversation™ Series for hundreds of individuals, women, men, and children as well as for leadership teams and employees within organizations and companies as diverse as financial institutions, construction companies, addiction recovery centers, and currently, as a publisher, editor, and Daring to Share Global storytelling and writing coach. The results are always the same, acute and cathartic personal awakenings that inspire confident action towards leading an authentic way of being. It is an amplified level of awareness that provides the ability to understand who we are as unique individuals to a degree whereby we are able to confidently make decisions in the moment or over a prolonged period of time that reiterate who we are as our authentic selves. Because we experience similar awakenings, we get to know each other from a more inclusive perspective and compassion arises, interactions soften and we become more respectful and humane.

This series is not only incredibly effective, but was developed to provide the ease of conversation in order to find clarity about what our next steps might be towards leading and living a truly authentic life. Conversation is a very powerful tool when used with the intention of honouring those who are willing to share their truth. When we respect others sharing, we are suddenly inspired to share our own truth with the same degree of self-respect and self-confidence. There is a mutual understanding of telling and listening. Deception dissipates and reciprocal trust is developed as we share how we feel and what we believe without being judged by the listener or by ourselves. It is during the uncertain times when seeking confirmation for our choices that we can follow through with them knowing our decisions are validated simply because we know ourselves so well.

What I find amazing is just how much clarity we are actually capable of achieving and that when we reach a point when we think we have conquered indecisiveness forever our mind is ready to strive for and seek even more truth. This is because being clear allows us to show up in line with what we truly believe, in other words, a little more authentically. With each added degree of clarity, we feel more at ease and this motivates us to raise the bar on showing up even more in line with our personal integrity. It is cathartic, feels amazing, and we want more. It's like a positive addiction with super-power side effects.

Not only is it imperative that we know ourselves, but as an ethical society, there is an obligation to get to know others and encourage them to be authentic within both their personal and professional lives. It is only when we understand each other's truths, that we are able to interact with one another in a way that is real. This clarity provides an understanding of our own and others' most detailed inner pieces including what motivates us, what we are passionate about, what triggers us, and how we want to feel and don't want to feel. This is when our true skills, talents, and genius shine through as humane collaboration.

It is my belief that we have a responsibility as human beings to not only know ourselves but also understand anyone we interact with, whether we choose to or not and especially when we fear them the most. We need to have conversations, whether comfortable or uncomfortable, that allow us to accumulate the information we need to be able to respond to others in a moral and ethical way. Deep knowing influences how we respond to others and any situation that comes our way. When we seek understanding, we develop compassion for ourselves and others and we are able to push judgment aside while simultaneously providing a sense of belonging and inclusion to everyone involved. What an incredible gift we have the ability to choose and is provided by the power of conversation!!

I have proudly been an Authentic Leadership Program and Conversation Facilitator trained by Founder, Tana Heminsley and ALG Trainer, Laura Mack since 2012. My pride comes from a place of intuitive knowing that the guidance I offered through this Conversation Series throughout the years provided my clients with a high degree of self-discovery and personal evolution. The vast understanding of self they achieved provided the level of self-awareness they needed in order to show up as their authentic selves with confidence and without hesitation. When we have an acute knowing of who we are from our inside out, we establish a natural ability to respond to people and the world from a place of authentic reasoning, compassion, love, human-kindness, and respect. The end result is that we make decisions inspired by a want to do the ethical thing in order to honour all involved, rather than, making decisions motivated by the need to be right in order to satisfy ourselves alone or our ego.

In a world where we are constantly reminded to be authentic, Tana's first book, *Awaken Your Authentic Leadership: Lead with Inner Clarity and Purpose*, along with its companion Authenticity Journal, provide you with ways to find clarity about what being authentic means to you. She systematically guides you through a process of self-discovery with compassion and ease as her practical approach offers the ability to find an understanding of your inner self, what serves you well, and what doesn't no matter what the circumstance.

Taking it one step further within the work you are about to embrace in this book, *Awaken Your Authentic Leadership: Authentic Leadership Conversations for Meaningful Connections*, Tana offers a personal guide through the tool of conversation with worksheets that inspire you to share your new authentic way of approaching and responding to life with everyone you meet. These well thought out conversations will support you with practical skills to use during times of indecisiveness that may present suddenly during fleeting moments or creep up gradually over extended periods of time. This collection of worksheets also serves as your professional go-to enabling you to consciously support members of your team as they delve into their unique and authentic way of being no matter what the scenario. Although sometimes uncomfortable, these impactful conversations naturally lead to empowered feelings of confidence, collaboration, community, and connection. This is what authentic leadership can genuinely look and feel like in all areas of life and Tana's approach makes it feel as natural and easy as it possibly can.

When we become more aware of who we are, we feel connected to something bigger than we ever imagined we are able. We naturally share this feeling with others and mutual understanding is inspired. An innate clarity about what our truth is comfortably manifests into actually *being* that truth and then the inspiration to discover and support the truth of others is created. Suddenly, this translates into honouring one another as we choose to show up as we've always yearned to while respecting everyone living on this planet, including ourselves. This is the magic of authenticity and what motivated Tana Heminsley to create this masterpiece that generates and preserves the truth and dignity of ourselves and others no matter where we are in our lives; we become human advocates of the most authentic kind.

Diana Reyers
Founder, Daring to Share Global™
www.daringtoshare.com

Introduction by Tana Heminsley

If you are lucky enough, you have a person in your life who you feel completely safe to share all your thoughts and fears with. If you are even more fortunate, this individual is a colleague at work or perhaps even your boss.

For many though, it doesn't feel comfortable letting their guard down and having real conversations — particularly at work. They are fearful of the repercussions of others disagreeing with them and the subsequent judgment and belief that work and personal life should stay completely separate. They wear a metaphorical mask and take on a persona they believe will make them successful, contorting themselves to fit into what they think other people want them to be… sometimes for their entire career.

This takes a lot of personal energy as the stress of conforming to others' expectations reduces resiliency. It creates risks for organizations as information is left out of discussions because extroverts dominate the discussion and introverts don't feel comfortable sharing their opinions. The result is that creativity is quashed as the level of healthy debate around ideas is confined to a mainstream or vanilla version.

Take a moment to think of one of the meetings you attend every day. The pace is frantic, there is too much to cover in the allotted time, and individuals talk over each other in order to move their political agendas forward. Everyone is unaware and disinterested in what is going on in the worlds of their colleagues because they just want to get the meeting done, get on to the next one, and then home to their family. Notice how stressful it feels in your body just to be reminded of this environment.

Now imagine that same meeting a second time — where everyone in the room understands and practices being authentic; genuine and the same in all parts of their life while being able to tap into their inner moral compass, particularly during stressful interactions. Those involved are comfortable speaking their minds and being real with each other. In addition, each person is self-aware, empathetic and able to self-manage when they become triggered. Everyone engages in lively, respectful debates as they speak their truth and stand up for their opinion even if it feels risky sharing it. The conversation is rich and the creativity and results vastly improve while the depth of relationships increases.

This is what authentic leadership conversations look like.

What is groundbreaking is how they feel — safe. Suddenly, those who used to walk on eggshells due to their fear of being real, are experiencing environments where employees feel comfortable to share their inner-most feelings and thoughts and they are able to flourish. These benefits, although sometimes difficult to describe, must not be underestimated because a strong foundation of trust leads to high-performing teams, raving customer fans, and resilient organizations — all of which contribute to bottom-line results.

This book is the third in the *Awaken Your Authentic Leadership* series. The first book, *Awaken Your Authentic Leadership: Lead with Inner Clarity and Purpose*, outlines what an authentic leader is, what the business case for being authentic is, and provides the nine-steps within the Authentic You™ Personal Planning System. It also lists concepts and examples for understanding and tools to complete deep self-reflections supporting you to step back at any time in your life while asking big questions such as, *Who am I? What am I meant to do with my life? How do I want to lead? What are the self-limiting beliefs getting in my way? And, how do I want to go forward during the next chapter in my leadership and life?*

The second book, *Awaken Your Authentic Leadership — Authenticity Journal*, provides the space you need to do this work — there are five separate sets of the *Personal Learning Journal*. These additional sets offer the opportunity for you to complete the *Personal Planning System* for the first time as well as iterations of the process in the future when your life and leadership require recalibration in answering life's call.

This third book provides a series of eighteen Action Worksheets forming the basis of an *Authentic Leadership Conversation™ Series*. The topics are outlined in detail over the next two pages. You can use the Action Worksheets in several ways:

As an individual leader:

- To build important well-known business skills such as facilitating a performance conversation or the process of delegation;
- To build newly recognized and emerging skills such as managing the inner critic or navigating transition and change;
- To build skills that support being authentic, including saying no and setting boundaries, living from the three centers of intelligence, and having authentic conversations;
- To transform your leadership by taking it to the next level by discovering new ways to lead when the old rules no longer resonate with you including skills such as how to cultivate joy at work.

And, as the leader of a team, department or organization:

- To build your team as you bring small groups together in conversation where each participant shares their self-reflections and learnings acquired from the Action Worksheets;
- To involve your employees as they choose the order the topics are discussed in;
- To create the space for real conversations to be practiced so that outside of these uniquely safe sessions your team can continue to use these skills with their colleagues and customers.

As the author, I took a few liberties — my style of writing is conversational and casual and I shared my experiences and stories in my own voice. I also added key insights and practices as materials for you to use to solve your day-to-day, work-related problems.

I included a few notes of context for each topic — what or who inspired me to write them as well as any final insights about how each one supports authentic leadership.

I also intentionally created duplication in each worksheet where I share the Arc of Intense Energy and how to use it to self-manage. This foundational skill is essential to focus on within each topic; while the concept is the same, the reflection and learnings are unique to each one.

I left space for you to write down your responses to the questions and self-reflections; it may be helpful to purchase a separate blank journal to make additional notes as well. This way you can use the worksheets over and over again as situations arise multiple times during your career.

And finally, as you learn the skills in the context of work, you will see benefits in all parts of your life. For example, if you are working on having difficult conversations at work, they may feel challenging in other parts of your life so the practice in one domain, supports skill building in both.

Thank you for doing this important work! The organizational world (and the world in general) needs some course corrections and together by cultivating authenticity and ethical approaches to leading, we can support it to be an even better place to be.

Tana Heminsley
Founder, Authentic Leadership Global™

How to Use This Book

One of the most important characteristics of an authentic leader is remembering and cultivating your ability to choose.

Authentic Leaders make intentional choices based on personal or inner clarity.
They take a proactive role in the creation of their life.
Each choice they make can be checked against what they know to be true.
If this is not aligned with their Authentic Self, their values or their vision, they choose differently.

~ Tana Heminsley, Awaken Your Authentic Leadership, © 2013, p 15.

There are several ways to use this book — it is important for you to make an intentional choice about your path — it is different for each person. You get to choose the approach that fits best based on what your needs are at this time.

Awaken Your Authentic Leadership — Authentic Conversations for Meaningful Connection can be used as a standalone workbook, or in conjunction with my first two books *Awaken Your Authentic Leadership: Lead with Inner Clarity and Purpose* and *Awaken Your Authentic Leadership — Authenticity Journal*. The first two books provide the global and business context, conceptual framework for understanding authenticity, and 9-step Authentic You™ Personal Planning System which is used to articulate and recalibrate your moral compass or inner guidance system. Once this guided period of self-reflection is complete, tangible goals are set for the next chapter of your life and areas for development are identified.

You can start with this book and complete it first, and then work through the other two; you can start with the other two and then work through this one; or you can work through them in parallel. There are lots of options. Go with what feels right for you at this time.

Assuming you will begin with this book, the 18 topics are listed in detail on the next few pages and while the number given to each topic is for ease of reference and use, the order is entirely random.

Below I have outlined the approach for you as an individual leader, and have also commented on working with an entire team.

To Grow as an Individual Leader

- **Choosing one topic** — Choose a topic that is up for you right now, a skill you are struggling with, or one you are curious to learn more about. Review and work through the Action Worksheet in detail in the context of the situation you are struggling with. Then in a few weeks or a month, review and reflect on what you are learning and what is different for you since the first time you worked through it. Ideally, work with a friend or colleague on the same topic and discuss it with each other. This will help to anchor the learnings for both of you. (Note: I have introduced the Arc of Intense Energy in the first Action Worksheet on page 17 and then refer you back to this foundational skill for authentic leadership in each of the other topics. If you would like an even more complete explanation of self-managing and The Arc of Intense Energy, please see my foundational book *Awaken Your Authentic Leadership: Lead with Inner Clarity and Purpose*, Chapter Six entitled Action.)

- **Creating a series** — Choose several topics that feel relevant for you over the next few months and create your own customized road map. Or, do this with a friend or colleague. Work through one Action Worksheet every few weeks or a month and have discussions about what you are learning in between.
- **Choosing a theme** — Identify an overriding challenge you are experiencing and use either option above to support your learning around this theme. For example, if you are having difficulty navigating the sheer volume of change you are experiencing, you can make this the theme for your learning. Then, choose the topics and work through them as they will support you to be better at navigating change. Your Inner Critic will need to be managed around how you think about change; learning to have difficult conversations, setting boundaries and saying no will support you to engage effectively with others about the change. Learning to listen to your three centers of intelligence will give you more perspective and ability to stay present through periods of intense change.

To Grow as a Member of a Team

Teams are as strong as each of their members. As one person evolves, so may the team.

Working with an experienced facilitator of Authentic Leadership Conversations™ is helpful when developing teams. For support and resources see www.leadauthentic.com.

As a reminder, long-term change of thoughts and behavior takes time and practice. These topics will create subtle shifts in perspective that build upon each other. It's always surprising to me how much I need to learn about the topic each time I return to work through it.

Enjoy the conversations.

Overview of Topics

The following table provides a detailed outline of the eighteen topics covered in the Authentic Leadership Conversation™ Series.

Topic #	Title	Topic Description
1	Understanding Authenticity and Emotional Intelligence	*What is emotional intelligence and how does it support me to lead from my authentic self?* *How does leading from authenticity and using emotional intelligence provide advantages in business?*
2	Navigating Transitions	*I thought my path in life was clear and now all the options feel a bit overwhelming!* *How do I move through unforeseen transitions in my leadership and my life?*
3	Managing the Inner Critic	*Who do I think I am?* *How do I manage my inner critic, my negative inner voice? And, how is my inner critic limiting my leadership and my life?*
4	Creating Work-life Balance	*I don't have the time!* *How do I balance everything in my life including leadership, family, aging parents, and fun?*
5	Having Difficult Conversations	*How can I say anything when I feel intimidated?* *How do I stay centered and clear during a difficult conversation when I feel intimidated by someone or when I am perceived as intimidating to others?*
6	Saying No and Setting Boundaries	*I just can't take that on!* *How do I learn to say No and feel ok with it?*
7	Integrating The Three Centers of Intelligence	*I live so much of the time in my head!* *How do I integrate the three centers of intelligence to improve my leadership and my life?*

8	Discovering New Models for Leadership	*I'm not comfortable with the old rules; they don't feel like a good fit for me anymore!* *How can I support organizational leadership being different in the 21st century? What needs to change?*
9	Having a Difficult Performance Conversation	*How can I say that?* *How do I have a difficult conversation at work or where I volunteer with an employee or contractor about her/his poor performance?*
10	Shifting Scarcity to Abundance Mindset	*When will I ever feel I have enough?* *How does a scarcity versus abundance mindset impact my leadership and my life?*
11	Leading and Living Congruent with Values	*That's a tricky one!* *How do I live congruent with my values, especially in difficult situations?*
12	Managing Conflict	*I am so uncomfortable with conflict!* *How do I develop my ability to manage conflict in my leadership and my life?*
13	Learning to Delegate	*I can do it myself!* *How do I delegate and feel ok with it?*
14	Receiving and Giving Feedback	*I don't know how or what to say!* *How can I give feedback that is meaningful and effective when it feels uncomfortable?*
15	Cultivating Joy at Work	*I want to experience joy and ease at work!* *How do I cultivate joy when I am so busy and overwhelmed at work?*

OVERVIEW OF TOPICS

16	Building Relationships Authentically	*Networking often feels phony for me!* *How can I connect with others in a genuine way while building my business?*
17	Having Effective Meetings	*I'm feeling overwhelmed!* *How do I conduct effective meetings when there seems to be so many of them?*
18	Having an Authentic Conversation	*I want to have Authentic Conversations!* *How can I take my mask off and be myself when it feels so vulnerable and scary?*

I was greatly impacted when I began learning about emotional intelligence through the work of Daniel Goleman. His Harvard Business Review Article entitled, *What Makes a Leader?* left a strong impression on me as I realized the potential for leaders to be able to manage their emotions, particularly during times of stress and intense pressure.

In addition to this, when Bill George came out with his book, *Discover Your True North*, it finally gave me the language to describe what I was trying to articulate as my philosophy of leadership — that being myself was difficult, yet at the same time, an empowering thing. It supported me to be free of the unhelpful aspects of my mind that I allowed to hold me back and cause me stress. This action worksheet brings the two related topics together and while there are many thought leaders in the field of both, I continue to come back to the work of these original authors.

It can be the first topic you work through or feel free to choose any topic that resonates with you in this moment. Whatever arises is the right skill for you to build at this time.

Understanding Authenticity and Emotional Intelligence

— Action Worksheet —

> **Topic Description:**
>
> *What is emotional intelligence and how does it support me to lead from my authentic self?*
>
> *How does leading from authenticity and using emotional intelligence provide advantages in business?*

The following worksheet will assist you to become more aware of authenticity and emotional intelligence as they relate to your leadership and your life. It will also support you to take the first steps to begin to lead and live with a bit more authenticity and emotional intelligence.

Authenticity Is:

- Being genuine and consistent in all parts of your life;
- Having the ability to choose your response in each moment after taking in information and interpreting it using the awareness of filters your personality may be creating through judgments, assumptions, stories, etc. as well as feeling and experiencing your emotions as they arise, rather than blocking them if they are too uncomfortable, and using your intuition to sense what may be unsaid and yet intended;
- Being able to manifest your leadership and your life daily in ways congruent with your authentic self or essence.

Outwardly, Authentic Leaders:[1]

- Are steady and confident in their presence — the leader is trusted;
- Have a reputation for being authentic and effective;
- Are willing to be vulnerable and seek real feedback in order to stay grounded;
- Are consistent in all parts of their life.

Internally, Authentic Leaders:

- Demonstrate a passion for their purpose[2];

---

1 Adapted from Bill George, Peter Sims, et al., Discovering Your Authentic Leadership, Harvard Business Review, February 2007.

2 Bill George, "Authentic Leadership: Rediscovering the Secrets to Creating Lasting Value, as cited by Bill George, et al. in Ibid, 2003.

- Are aware of their impact on others;
- Are aware of their automatic patterns, beliefs, and habits that may limit their leadership, or ask feedback from others to support them to continue developing awareness;
- Recognize the value of diversity of perspectives, both the intuitive and the logical as well as the operational and the strategic.

Emotional Intelligence (EI)

Daniel Goleman's article, *What Makes a Leader?* introduced a model of emotional intelligence with five skills *that enable the best leaders to maximize their own and their followers' performance*. These include:

- Self-awareness — Knowing one's emotions, strengths, weaknesses, drivers, values, and goals and their impact on others;
- Self-regulation — Controlling or redirecting disruptive emotions and impulses;
- Motivation — Being driven to achieve for the sake of achievement; also balancing external with internal, intrinsic motivations;
- Empathy — Considering others' feelings, especially when making decisions;
- Social Skill — Managing relationships to move people in desired directions[3].

Emotional Intelligence supports authenticity and improved business performance in several ways:

- When leaders are self-aware, they have more choice in how they deal with situations. They are able to choose to step back in the moment and move beyond their normal, default ways of managing conversations and relationships — particularly when a new response is required. They can be authentic. Emotionally intelligent leaders call on their values and their awareness of their strengths and weaknesses to successfully navigate new or stressful situations or those with people from different cultures;
- Emotionally intelligent leaders can motivate and engage employees as they take the time to build strong relationships through listening and understanding the other peoples' perspectives. Leaders come into a relationship with positional credibility — they are the boss — which creates a power imbalance that can intimidate employees. Mature leaders are aware of this and practice role modeling authenticity;
- Emotionally intelligent leaders are able to integrate their personal life with their careers and create situations that are respectful of both personal values and business needs. They are more successful as a result of their authenticity in all parts of their lives — they are consistently the same person whether at the office or at home.

Authentic Leadership Improves Results

Authentic Leaders with strong EI are more effective as they exhibit the following:

- Stronger leadership through trust-based relationship building as leaders are able to see old patterns that limit them from connecting with others and they work towards building skills to develop long-term, trust-based relationships;
- Proactive resolution of business challenges before they become a problem as leaders become

---
3 Daniel Goleman, "What Makes a Leader?" Harvard Business Review, 1998.

better active listeners, are more open to possibilities, less defensive and more available and able to have difficult conversations;
- Grounded confidence which creates a more stimulating and engaging environment for their team;
- Ability to manage the increasing volume and complexity of demands as leaders are more able to maintain perspective, cultivate ease, and focus their efforts on the critical items at the right level. They practice developing balance through adjusting their schedule, priorities, and the way they engage their team rather than micromanaging them in order to be rejuvenated at the end of the week versus being exhausted.

The team is more effective and works in an environment with role models for being authentic themselves:
- Team members respond positively as leaders are able to be vulnerable with them which makes the leaders more approachable and available;
- Team members know where they stand in terms of performance on a day-to-day basis as leaders are more confident having difficult conversations;
- Team members are more engaged as leaders are able to see old patterns of micro-managing and control, and they build the skill to involve others and let these go.

The company is successful and sustainable over the long term:
- Better business decisions are made as leaders create a platform for diversity of opinions encouraging thoughtful dialogue; they are not as hasty to make decisions before drawing out the different perspectives from the team;
- Decreased risks and increased transparency as leaders are able to ask for help when they need it versus trying to deal with issues on their own and not involving others early enough to reduce the risk. For some leaders this can be a profound shift.

The community and world are better as a result:
- Authentic leaders create a win-win-win situation for the individual, company and the world as individuals bring their passion to their leadership; they create environments where team members can be themselves and feel safe to approach others in difficult situations and the ripple effect moves outside the company to customers and families.

Cultivating Authenticity in Leadership

The basis for authentic leadership is that to be successful, leaders must find ways to learn about themselves, including what motivates and challenges them and who they are when they are leading from their authentic selves. They then need to incorporate practices, systems, and feedback to support them in leading from authenticity more of the time:

- Notice to see your racing mind and practice being present to build capacity for choice in how you respond;
- Understand your personality type using assessments such as the Enneagram, Myers Briggs, Insights, etc. and learn to let go of old, automatic patterns and beliefs that may no longer serve you;
- Seek out real feedback from others with whom you know you can be your authentic self;
- Understand who you are when at your best with clarity about what your authentic-self qualities

are, what your intention or gift in the world is, what your values are, what your vision is, and how you want to translate these into your leadership principles;
- Keep your personal foundation strong (exercise, nutrition, spirituality, fun, balance, etc.) as it can take more energy to be authentic versus going with the flow;
- Be open to meaningful connections and support from others by finding a community of support where you can be your true self versus isolating and trying to do it all on your own.

ACTION STEPS

Read the following articles:
- Bill George, Peter Sims, et al., *Discovering Your Authentic Leadership*, Harvard Business Review, February 2007.
- Daniel Goleman, *What Makes a Leader?*, Harvard Business Review, 1998.

Reflections
Reflect on what you are learning about leadership and yourself as a leader. Write your thoughts here:

Decide on one thing you can do differently as a result of what you have learned:

Practices

Develop awareness of when you are being authentic and when you are reacting from auto-pilot; using old automatic patterns and beliefs that may no longer be needed in your life

The first step is to become aware of your authentic self, who you are when at your best versus who you are when responding from automatic beliefs and habits.

Over the next six months begin a section in a journal or create a document and call it *noticing authenticity in myself as a leader*. For fifteen minutes at the end of each week, check in with yourself and reflect on when you brought authenticity to your leadership, being self-aware and real while living congruently with your values and ethics.

Notice how it felt both physically and emotionally to be authentic and what the responses of others were to you in the situation.

Notice other times when you felt out of alignment with who you are when you wore the mask that some people feel is necessary to fit in and succeed. Reflect on what the difference is between the two situations. How do you know? Reflect on what you are learning and what you can do differently as a result.

Taking action to live authentically more of the time

Practice being vulnerable to support others to feel comfortable sharing their opinion in particular when you might not agree. For the next three months, once a week, when in a meeting with members of your team, and when there is a new challenge to resolve, tell the team you don't have all the answers and would like their ideas for the solution. Say it in a way you are comfortable with.

Notice how it feels to be vulnerable with others. Also, notice how they respond when they are permitted to not have all the answers.

Reflect on what you learned and what you can do differently as a result.

The Arc of Intense Energy

During stressful situations your body will go into flight, flight or freeze. When this occurs, it can be difficult to stay present to your thoughts and emotions that feel like a wave of intense energy which builds and builds and then eventually dissipates. This experience is depicted below as an arc.

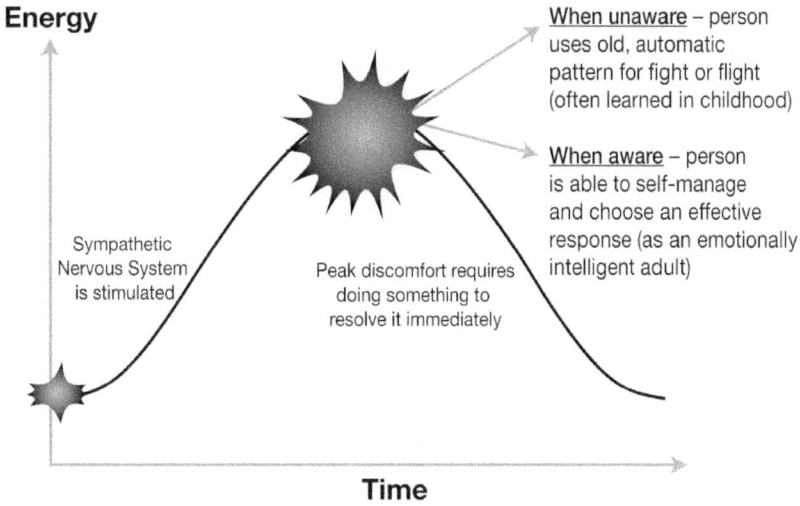

When you are unaware of your thoughts and emotions, at the peak of the arc, your body will not be able to tolerate the discomfort and your mind will do anything to resolve the tension. Often this means you react using old, unhelpful automatic patterns of thoughts and behaviours, to deal with situations. Remember a time when you lashed out at a colleague or family member and afterwards you wished you would not have said that. These are the situations I am describing.

When you have a practice of cultivating awareness, you will navigate with that inner guidance system. You can begin by paying attention; noticing the energy or discomfort intensifying in the body. As this occurs, practice relaxing your shoulders and belly and deepen and slow your breathing. This will allow you to feel the emotions as they arise, notice your thoughts and discern if they are aligned with your values or just old, unhelpful messages. When you learn to discern which is true and right, you will be able to maintain your perspective and choose a response that is appropriate, and authentic, for the situation at hand.

This is an advanced skill found in an emotionally mature and authentic individual and takes time and practice to be able to master.

Arc of Intense Energy Reflection

Reflect on the topic of this chapter — being authentic and emotionally intelligent. Answer the following questions in order to understand how the arc is showing up for you:

What is your old, automatic pattern when triggered? For example, *When I am triggered by a person who I feel is being aggressive towards me, I begin to contract my shoulders and stop sharing my opinion.*

What is a new behaviour, belief or attitude you would like to choose instead? For example, *When I am triggered by a person who I feel is being overly aggressive towards me, I become more confident and articulate my opinion in a clear, strong voice.*

When you practice self-managing, remember your responses to these two questions. Practice using the new behaviour, belief or attitude as your response when triggered.

Closing Reading

*The question is not why are you so infrequently the person you really want to be.
The question is why do you so infrequently want to be the person you really are.*[4]

How would your leadership be different if you were able
to be the person you really are more of the time?

Relax into your authenticity and live this day with just a little more ease.
~ Tana Heminsley

---

[4] Adapted from Oriah Mountain Dreamer, "The Dance — Moving to the Deep Rhythms of Your Life", p 7, 2001.

There are many overwhelmed and overworked leaders today.

Navigating all the transitions and the sheer volume of change they experience each day on the job can be supported by an authentic approach — turning attention to the inner landscape and staying connected to the deep knowing of your inner moral compass.

When you use this lens to be intentional and to guide your steps, in often unstable and unknown ground, you will be guided intuitively towards the right and ethical way to move forward.

Navigating Transitions

— Action Worksheet —

> **Topic Description:**
> *I thought my path in life was clear and now all the options feel a bit overwhelming! How do I move through unforeseen transitions in my leadership and my life?*

Transitions in our lives take many forms and can be startling when we are not prepared for them. They are a time of being in the *not knowing* of life, and for those of us who like to be in control, the experience can range from exciting to mildly unsettling or even devastating. Transitions are also the time for new and meaningful opportunities to emerge.

In our fast-paced world, the saying, *the only constant in life is change*, is becoming more and more the case. We can resist it, or we can learn to be OK with ambiguity and transition. If we make the choice to go with the flow and build the skills and capacity to navigate unforeseen transitions in our leadership and our lives, we can reduce our stress levels and the amount of time and energy we spend worrying and trying to maintain the status quo. In addition, we can open to possibilities for the future that we may not have ever considered in the past.

The following worksheet will assist you to become more aware of how to navigate transitions, and change in general and how this can be a support for your leadership and your life. It will also support you to take the first steps in beginning to lead and live with a bit more capacity to be with the ambiguity that is the constant in the world today.

There are three thoughts to consider regarding navigating transitions. Here in Canada, when we were children learning how to venture into the unknown of crossing a busy street, we were given guidance that is equally applicable now:

Stop, Look, and Listen:

- Stop and Breathe — take the time to make space for transition in the *busy-ness* of our lives;
- Look within — get to know our self again and articulate what is truly important to us;
- Listen to what arises — practice patience and listen to what comes as we re-discover our dreams and open to new possibilities.

Stop — take the time to make space for transition in the *busy-ness* of our lives:

- Our culture values busy. Superwomen and men are applauded. We may keep ourselves busy in order to avoid the uncomfortable feelings a transition can bring up for us. There is a paradox in times of transition — in order to go forward, we must first learn to slow…
- Slowing may mean learning to make space in our very full lives. Transitions take time and emotional energy and require creating white space on the canvas of our lives as we prepare

for a new painting for the future. It can be helpful to take things off our *to-do* lists. It may mean stepping down from boards or volunteer activities or at least considering the possibility. It may mean learning how to value ourselves enough by prioritizing self-care for a period of time (for some it might be for the first time in their lives) as we enter a period of transition.

Look — look within to get to know yourself again and articulate what is truly important to you:

- We get the results in our lives that we receive because of how we learned to see the world and live within it;
- When something about our world changes and our current ways of being no longer work for us, we get a wake-up call. We may experience trauma such as divorce, death, loss of our job, etc., we may receive unwanted health-related news like developing type two diabetes or seeing our cholesterol levels skyrocket, we may near the stage of retirement, or we may accomplish everything we always wanted and then realize there must be something more. We begin asking ourselves questions — *What is life really about? What is my purpose? What is next? What is the reason I am meant to be here on this earth?*
- Change brings an opportunity to look deeply within our life story and current way of living and to look at who we are and what is important to us. It gives us pause to discover what is truly important — without the mask of ego and the old ways of thinking about the world, those old patterns of thought or behaviour that may no longer serve us. Transition provides the opportunity for us to choose to be who we are without the *shoulds* of our culture; *I should want to be successful, I should want a family, I should be a certain way in order to fit in, I should want to accumulate more stuff than anyone around me*, etc.;
- Whatever the *shoulds* of your life are, can you imagine what it would be like to live in a way that is aligned with who you truly are?
- During transition, who we are can become cloudy as we move forward tentatively and on shaky ground. Leaders who leave the corporate world when they reach the point in their career when they want to do something different can experience a time of questioning — *If not the executive, who am I?*
- What can be helpful is to take the time to relax into who we are and to learn about the next layers or patterns of thought and behavior that it's time to let go of. By letting go of assumptions about how life should be lived, new options can be seen about how we might want to organize how we want to live going forward. Self-awareness can provide more choice when answering the question, *What's next?*
- We can spend some time gathering information from friends and family to support articulating who we are when at our best — what our unique gifts are as human beings. We can become clear about our values and our vision for life and how these translate into our leadership style and practices, our goals, and our internal development as individuals;
- This is when we are able to take a fresh look at where we might want to set different boundaries for what is acceptable and what is not — reflect on any situations in our life where we are not living congruently with our values;
- We can learn to integrate our thinking mind with our emotions and intuition. Often in the business world, we spend much of our time using our thinking mind and we are not always encouraged to follow our intuition. We cut ourselves off from our bodies and our ability to sense what else is going on with unspoken agendas and non-verbal undercurrents that show up in the room. By slowing and integrating the head, heart, and gut, we bring additional information

to our decision-making and day-to-day way of being that is more complete and allows us to live congruent with who we are;
- We can do whatever it takes — with a guide or on our own — to get *unstuck* and see something different than we ever imagined.

Listen — listen to what arises — practice patience and listen to what comes as we re-discover our dreams and open to new possibilities:
- Transitions take time and developing self-awareness of our patterns around patience and impatience as well as developing compassion for ourselves can be helpful. Trying to force a new way versus opening to what feels right can take us in entirely different directions;
- In addition, being open to support and community as well as keeping our foundational practices in place (nutrition, exercise, fun, spirituality, etc.) support us as we navigate this journey.

ACTION STEPS

Develop awareness of the specifics of your reaction to transitions and change

The first step is to become aware of how you react and think about transition or change. Complete the following exercise over the next month:
- Start a new page in your journal and begin an inquiry for the next month — an inquiry is continuous intentional reflection about a topic with the process being more important than the end *answer* that emerges. Reflect on the following questions for ten minutes weekly. Answer all of them each week and notice the layers of awareness that arise. Reflect on what you are learning about yourself and what you can do differently as a result.

Reflections

How do you feel about transition and change?

What would it be like if you could remain centered and clear in the wake of change — to be open to dancing with what comes?

How are you taking care of yourself? Transitions can take energy.

What beliefs and behaviors may be blocking you from seeing new possibilities for what is next?

What support can you put in place as you navigate this transition?

Practices

Practices are things we do over and over again, physically, to develop new behaviours or habits. Complete the following practice for the next three months:

- At the end of each week, make a list of how you spent your days — for each activity notice where your energy builds and where it drains. Ask yourself, *For the sake of what am I doing this activity?* Begin to notice what experiences are truly important to you and what it is about the activity that makes it so meaningful. Reflect on what you are learning and what you can do differently as a result. Write your responses here:

Arc of Intense Energy Reflection

Refer to the diagram and description of the Arc of Intense Energy on page 17. Reflect on the topic of this chapter — navigating transitions. Answer the following questions in order to understand how the arc is showing up for you:

What is your old, automatic pattern when triggered? For example, *when I am triggered around change, I resist and do not budge from my current position as the only way forward.*

What is a new behaviour, belief or attitude you would like to choose instead? For example, *when I am triggered around change, I breathe through the resistance I notice, and seek out more information from reliable sources so I can adapt my thinking and behavior to the new reality.*

Practice self-managing through the arc when you are learning about this topic. Begin by paying attention; noticing the energy or discomfort intensifying in the body. As this occurs, practice relaxing your shoulders and belly and deepen and slow your breathing.

This will allow you to feel the emotions as they arise, notice your thoughts and discern if they are aligned with your values or just old, unhelpful messages.

When you learn to discern which is true and right, you will be able to maintain your perspective and choose a response that is appropriate, and authentic, for the situation at hand.

Remember your responses to these two questions. Practice using the new behaviour, belief or attitude as your response when triggered.

After a few weeks of practicing, reflect on what you are learning and how you will adjust your thoughts and behaviours as a result.

Closing Reading

*The winds of change blow through our life, sometimes gently,
sometimes like a tropical storm.*

*Yes, we have resting places — time to adjust to another level of living, time to get our balance,
time to enjoy the rewards. We have time to catch our breath.*

But change is inevitable...

*Sometimes, when the winds of change begin to rustle, we're not certain
the change is for the better.*

We may call it stress or a temporary condition, certain we'll be restored to normal.

Sometimes we resist.

*We tuck our head down and buck the wind, hoping that things will quickly calm down,
get back to the way things were.*

Is it possible we're being prepared for a new "normal"?[5]

---

5   Melody Beattie, The Language of Letting Go, p 106, Accepting Change, April 19th

I wrote this topic first and, after many years, it remains the most popular of all of the Authentic Leadership Conversation™ topics.

I started a Women's Leadership Dinner Series and asked a potential client what her wish list was for topics as well as where she wanted to meet to discuss them with others. I was facilitating retreats off the coast of Vancouver, B.C. and she said, as a new mother, she couldn't take the time away from her family to attend the retreats, but she wanted to meet regularly, in town, over dinner after work.

And, so the writing of these topics began.

Managing the inner critic is foundational to being an authentic leader as, in the words of the New Ventures West Integral Coach Instructor, Sarita Chawla, *The critic keeps us on the straight and narrow to not becoming who we truly are*.

Awareness of unhelpful aspects of how the mind naturally works and the ability to override or manage them, support living aligned with our truth and authenticity more of the time.

Managing the Inner Critic

— Action Worksheet —

> **Topic Description:**
>
> *Who do I think I am?*
>
> *How do I manage my inner critic, my negative inner voice?*
> *And, how is my inner critic limiting my leadership and my life?*

The following worksheet will assist you to become more aware of the *inner critic* as it relates to your leadership and your life. It will also support you to take the first steps to begin to lead and live with a bit more freedom from your inner critic.

Things to Consider About the Inner Critic:

- The critic will always be there — as you become aware of it, it may become even louder;
- It is possible to shift how you experience the inner critic when it comes up and to reduce its impact on your life;
- Compassion is the gateway — both for others and for yourself.

The critic will always be there

What is the inner critic? How does it show at work? At home?

- While I'm not sure when I first became aware of my inner critic, I do know that I've carried this voice around for a long time. I remember asking a woman who I admired, considered quite successful and was getting support from a few years ago how she stopped her critic. She told me that it was still alive and well, and in fact, sometimes became so loud when she entered into something new that she had to have a conversation with it and partner with it, override it and then go on;
- I also remember an incredibly successful instructor at a leadership program I attended in San Francisco telling us that each time she was about to start the program, her critic was so strong that she continued to believe no one would show up. And each time people did. And each time she was incredibly successful;
- Over the years, my critic has asked me, *Who do you think you are to try doing that?* and told me, *You are so ugly* and *You're such a fraud — they are going to find out*. When I facilitate leadership sessions it says, *They are going to think you're crazy* and *They already know this stuff — it's not new or useful*. Does the critical nature of your inner voice sound familiar?

It is possible to shift how we experience the critic

- The inner critic doesn't have to be an unwanted guest who comes to our door and stays way past their welcome. We can build the capacity to see the inner critic for what it is — just a thought — one that will last a few seconds — and then, go away;

- For some, it's been there for so long it becomes their orientation towards themselves and they begin to believe it can only be this way. I've come to realize that we have the ability to choose how we see the world. In each moment, we can decide how we feel about the situation and ourselves;
- I remember a good friend telling me that he is now able to see his critic as a little green gremlin who appears at his front door. In the past, it would sit down in his living room and, in a very loud voice, yell out nasty messages. Now, he sees the gremlin enter the house, go through the hallway and kitchen, and right out the back door. It no longer has the hold on him that it once did.

Compassion is the gateway – both for others and for yourself

- It's a thought that just lasts a few seconds or longer if we obsess about it and replay it over and over;
- In its basic form, the inner critic is the internalization of the messages we received as children and young adults from others who influenced us at that time;
- If we allow ourselves to manage it, we can learn to step into our full power more of the time and in spite of it;
- It can be managed as we learn to see it, keep it in perspective, laugh at it at times, scream at it at times in our heads, and practice letting it go – the volume gets louder or softer at times depending on how well we are and whether or not we have our foundational practices in place;
- I met very few without one; for some, it is sensed as a feeling rather than hearing it as a voice and some have an entire *board of directors* of inner critics going on within;
- Compassion for self and others is very helpful – perhaps through a loving-kindness meditation. Also, a community of support to discuss it, to learn from, and to share experiences with can be really wonderful.

Managing the Inner Critic

How does the inner critic impact us at work?

- When in meetings, the inner critic can stop us from speaking; it may say, *That's stupid, don't say it*;
- Again, in meeting with others, it can stop us from being open to their ideas; it may say, *That's wrong; it can only be one way – this way*;
- When working with others, it can stop us from being empathetic or compassionate towards them, a foundational competency of emotional maturity verses checking out what is going on for them today; it may say, *He's so aggressive, or she's so condescending* when the reason may be that they've had a really bad morning and being empathetic would calm the situation down.

What can we do to manage the inner critic?

- Through developing self-awareness, learning to rebalance our thoughts, and opening to a new voice, one of compassion and empathy, over time, we are able to turn down the volume of the critic and let go of its hold. This provides us with more choice and we can respond verses react;
- This is the focus of the worksheet we've created for those who like to go to action and do something differently as a result of these self-reflections.

How can we use compassion and empathy to support managing the inner critic?
- When I sense a strong inner critic in someone, it is usually a result of them experiencing self-talk during our conversations. The example I experience the most is when someone is given a compliment and immediately responds in a way that diminishes the intent of it. It's as if they feel it would be arrogant to allow the kind words to really sink in;
- Are you able to accept positive feedback at work? Are you able to really take it in and feel it? What about negative feedback? Do you know what the ratio of positive to negative needs to be to balance the impact of the negative in order to hear the positive? The ratio is 5:1. It's much easier to see the negative and it takes effort and practice to have choice in the moment to see a balanced perspective. But it can be done;
- Negative self-talk can be an indication of how compassionate we are with ourselves, which can then show up through how we treat others;
- It involves projection (what we believe, we sense in someone else or we project on to them) which then arises when we judge others; it may be a projection on them of what would be too painful to see in ourselves. *I can't be like that — it must be them*;
- How does it show up at work? How does it show up when you are working with others? Is there someone you have a particularly hard time working with? What is it about them that you are having difficulty with? Can you see this in yourself at times as well? What would it be like for you to be empathic with the person verses judgmental? How might this change the dynamic in the moment?
- When we learn to see the goodness in people and have compassion for them, to stay with our curious-self verses going to judgment, we are actually giving ourselves a gift as it is through learning to be compassionate with them that we learn to be kinder to ourselves;
- If the word compassionate is loaded for you, or if you have judgments about it and it feels uncomfortable, think about it as empathy — the ability to step into other's shoes and understand their experience. While you may not totally agree with what they believe, you can still endeavor to understand it;
- Through a shift in how we think about the world and ourselves, we can learn to live with the inner critic, some even say partner with, so it can allow us to be who we truly are and not who we have learned to be.

ACTION STEPS

Exercises to develop awareness of the specifics of your inner critic and take action to live in spite of your inner critic:
- The first step is to become aware of your inner critic — what it sounds like, what it looks like. Do you have just one critical voice, or do you have an entire committee? And, most importantly, determine the messages it is telling you;
- Because the inner critic may have been a part of your mind for a very long time, it may always be there. What we are trying to do with these exercises is to support you in seeing it for what it is, and to grow your capability to step back when you hear it, to keep your perspective, and

to minimize the impact it is having on your leadership and your life. Is the critic correct? Or, it may be a *tape* that plays over and over again from an earlier part of your life that no longer serves you;
- Some leaders sense this critical mood as a feeling in their body rather than verbally as words. If this is the case for you, it may be helpful to reflect on these feelings and the messages they provide you.

Reflections
Answer the Following Questions to Get to Know Your Inner Critic a Bit Better:
What does your inner critic sound like? Is it high pitched, low volume, soft, loud, etc.?

What does your inner critic(s) look like? Is it an angry schoolmaster, a monster, a troll, etc.?

What are the messages your inner critic is saying to you — *That's stupid! Who do you think you are? You're ugly! What a failure!?* Note that this may take time and be different in different situations.

MANAGING THE INNER CRITIC

How are these messages impacting your leadership? My life?

What would I be like if you lived free of this inner critical voice? What would it feel like? How much less energy would I expend on worry?

What are you learning about yourself? What one thing can you do differently as a result?

Practices

When you begin working with the inner critic you learn to create a different way of thinking about your life — imagine re-hardwiring your brain to a new way that may feel uncomfortable if your automatic pattern is to adopt a negative perspective most the time. Give yourself a chance. Remember, like so many others, it will take time and self-compassion as you begin using practices to become aware of what you choose to pay attention to and begin rebalancing your thoughts.

Once a week, see if you can catch your inner critic in the act. As soon as you become aware, take five minutes to complete the following exercise. It is important to rebalance the thoughts as soon after as possible in order to minimize the energy you spend on the situation, and to begin retraining your mind.

- Write down exactly what it is saying to you and how you feel as a result. Your inner critic is saying the following right now: For example, *That person thought what you said was stupid — didn't you see her furrowed brow?*

- Write down an alternative, more balanced message for yourself. A more balanced way for you to think about this situation is the following: For example, *I noticed that the person I was talking to had a furrowed brow — they may have been thinking of a question about what I was presenting.*

MANAGING THE INNER CRITIC

- Notice how each of these statements feels when you re-read them. It is important to begin to notice how the inner critic impacts you physically so you can learn to notice it, let it go, and move on.
  When you read the inner critic's statement you feel:

  When you read the more balanced statement you feel:

- Ask yourself how you would interpret this situation from authentic self, without the impacts of your critical voice. Listen to your intuition regarding what your truth is in the situation. Re-interpret it using this perspective. Then, notice how it feels to let your inner critic go…for now. For example, *I am learning that I am an extrovert and as such I process by talking things through. Others may be introverts, and they may process by thinking things through before they respond. This person may be processing and when they do, they furrow their brow. I notice my inner critic and the assumptions it causes me to make; I need to check them out before I come to a conclusion. I need to ask the person next time I see him/her what was on his/her mind when I noticed their furrowed brow.*

  When you listen to your intuition and are aware of your inner critic or the more emotionally mature way to interpret this situation, you find the more balanced or objective way to think about this situation is:

Checking Out Projections

One of the things that can be occurring when we are critical of others and make judgments, is that our inner critic is being misplaced onto them. This is called projection. We project something onto the person we judge when it is too uncomfortable to see the same in ourselves. For example, thinking that person is so loud and talks too much verses having personal awareness that I can be loud and talk too much as well. Becoming aware of these parts of ourselves and accepting them can be helpful to develop compassion or empathy for ourselves and others.

Reflections About Projections

When you have a hard time with a person and notice your judgments arise, answer the following questions:

- What is it about this person you are having such a hard time with? Specifically, it is the following: For example, *He is so controlling and is micromanaging me on this project.*

- Using the phrase, *I am*, substitute the behaviours that bother you about the other person and write a statement about yourself: For example, *I am so controlling and I micromanage others at times.*

    I am also…

- Write an example of a time you experienced this in yourself:
  An example of when I was like this was…

- Reflect on how having more empathy, one of the foundational competencies of emotional intelligence, can support you in your leadership and your life.

Once we realize that we are all just trying to be the best we can be and we are perfect including our imperfections, we can have more compassion or empathy for ourselves and others.

In the Moment Inner Critic Management:

- When we have an orientation to the critical, it helps to develop a different inner voice — one of compassion. For the next six months, whenever you are meeting with someone and you notice your judgments arising, practice staying curious with the person and staying connected. Notice how it feels verses other times when your thoughts immediately go to judgment and criticism. Notice how the person responds in each situation and how it feels for you. How can this support you to have compassion for yourself as a leader? Compassion for others? What can you do differently as a result?
- In the moment when you catch your inner critic at play, notice it for what it is — just one of the many thoughts that occupy your mind today. Laugh and say, *Oh, that's interesting*, and let it go. By giving the inner critic less *air play* we give it less energy and it dissipates more quickly.

Arc of Intense Energy Reflection

Refer to the diagram and description of the Arc of Intense Energy on page 17. Reflect on the topic of this chapter — managing the inner critic. Answer the following questions in order to understand how the arc is showing up for you:

What is your old, automatic pattern when triggered? Where is your inner critical voice triggering you? For example, *when I am triggered by someone telling me how to do something, I feel shame as my critic sends the message that my way is not good enough.*

What is a new behaviour, belief or attitude you would like to choose instead? For example, *when I am triggered by someone telling me how to do something, I notice shame arising as my critic sends the message that my way is not good enough, and I either set a boundary in a respectful way, or let it go knowing that it's just my critic trying to get in the way.*

Practice self-managing through the arc when you are learning about this topic. Begin by paying attention; noticing the energy or discomfort intensifying in the body. As this occurs, practice relaxing your shoulders and belly and deepen and slow your breathing.

This will allow you to feel the emotions as they arise, notice your thoughts and discern if they are aligned with your values or just old, unhelpful messages.

When you learn to discern which is true and right, you will be able to maintain your perspective and choose a response that is appropriate, and authentic, for the situation at hand.

Remember your responses to these two questions. Practice using the new behaviour, belief or attitude as your response when triggered.

After a few weeks of practicing, reflect on what you are learning and how you will adjust your thoughts and behaviours as a result.

Resources

Loving What Is, Byron Katie.

Taming Your Gremlin, Rick Carson.

Closing Reading

As we learn to be present to our lives and open to the moment, miracles begin to happen.

One of the greatest miracles is that we can drop a habit that has plagued us for many years in a minute.

When we are fully present, the old habit lets go and we are no longer the same.

To experience the healing of our oldest and deepest wounds through the action of awareness is the miracle we can all count on.

If we follow this map of the soul into the depths of our hearts, hatred will turn into compassion, rejection into acceptance, and fear into wonder.[6]

---

[6] Don Richard Riso and Russ Hudson, The Wisdom of the Enneagram, p 41, 1999.

While many leaders no longer use the language of work-life balance, I have found it useful to think of this fleeting state as just that — a dance in life requiring constant balance. Life will change with each day and each chapter, and it is very helpful to cultivate a perspective that you have some control over it, particularly during overwhelm.

When each week or each month is seen as a practice, and with a long-term horizon, hope is given as you get better at dancing in the midst of busy-ness; you become able to do something to re-center and maintain your authentic perspective. This muscle gets stronger over time and balance is seen for what it is — a choice in how to see the situation as well as the taking of steps immediately to regain just a little bit more control.

Many leaders have become aware that this topic is foundational to long-term success and resiliency. As one who burned out several times before learning how to master it, I wanted to share with others what I found helpful.

Creating Work-Life Balance

— Action Worksheet —

> **Topic Description:**
>
> *I don't have the time!*
>
> *How do I balance everything in my life including leadership, family, aging parents, and fun?*

Use the following worksheet to assist you in understanding your work-life balance and taking the first steps to having *just a little bit more* balance in your life as well as to make adjustments when you are feeling out of balance. When developing your plan, reflect on the following questions and complete the exercises as well as consider what support and conversations you may need to have in order to actively practice balance going forward.

Things to Consider About What Balance Is:

- A choice we make in how we see the world;
- A *muscle* we can strengthen over time;
- A life-long practice;
- A learning to live authentically in each part of our life.

Balance is a Choice We Make in How We See the World

Think of a hurricane where the storm of life frantically whirls and inside the clouds there is the eye. It is calm in the eye but it doesn't mean that the storm has stopped or slowed in intensity — on the contrary, the storm may continue for some time.

This concept is discussed in a book called *Slowing Down to the Speed of Life*. The authors describe two modes of thinking — the processing, analytical or task mode and the free-flow mode described as the creative intelligence or effortless thinking.[7] They talk about how important it is to learn to balance and live in both modes in order to be more effective leaders. The western culture values and rewards the *getting things done* mode of processing, so we learn to spend a large part of our lives living in this way of thinking. When we re-learn to spend time in the free-flow mode, we can tap more fully into our creativity, wisdom and original thinking.

Up until about two years ago, I had no idea that I was living in the frantic. I remember at its worst, I was sleeping about three hours a night and sending emails to the team at 4:00 in the morning. That was a good day. On a bad day, I remember getting up at 12:30… a.m.

I had no idea how out of control I was until a friend sat me down and said, *You look like you have a*

---

[7] Richard Carlson and Joseph Bailey, Slowing Down to the Speed of Life — How to create a more peaceful, simpler life from the Inside out, pp. 11-15.

huge weight on your shoulders — you know you don't have to do it all, you can ask for help. I remember thinking she was crazy, not wanting to hear the message and actually being angry with her. I thought, *How dare she?* And now, when I look back, I am so thankful.

I have learned to choose to live life from a place of the eye of the storm and to step into the *busy-ness* when I need to and to step back out to rejuvenate myself. It wasn't easy and it was very uncomfortable at times. I had to relearn how to slow my central nervous system and I had no idea what the free-flow mode of thinking was. I thought that if I wasn't *doing* or what I called *cranking*, I was being unproductive and I felt guilty.

And so, my journey of awareness continued. The stakes got high enough that I knew it was time to shift how I thought about and practiced balance.

It's taken support and several years for me to feel like I have a balanced life. Consistent foundational practices including meditation have been my savior. A simple daily sitting practice during the week has helped me become aware of my racing mind, develop the ability in a new or stressful situation to stop, breathe, notice my mind, get perspective and collect my thoughts. In the past, I struggled to maintain my foundational practices for wellness — running, yoga, journaling, annual nutritional cleanses — these were the first things to go when I got busy and had to get things done, which was more often the case than not.[8]

Balance is a Muscle We Learn to Strengthen Over Time

I worked with a great leader, a CEO of a multibillion-dollar firm, who demonstrated to me that balance is possible even when there are so many possibilities for how to spend our time; family, friends, careers, parents, projects, positions on boards, work, exercise and training… we each have many, many things we can choose to fill our time.

One difference between those who have balance and those who don't and that you can get a sense about them when you meet them, is that they are calm and centered, and while they may be busy, they are not anxious or overwhelmed, at least not a lot of the time. They have figured out what it takes to live life from a place where they can see the frantic and either choose not to be in it or choose when to be in it and when to step back to regain perspective. They are able to care for themselves, manage stress effectively, and be consistent in their foundation as a person with the caveat that there are times when balance goes away. These leaders have learned to notice when this happens, to navigate tradeoffs and return to a sense of balance more quickly than those who have not.

Long-term stress has many implications; here are a few signs of stress in thinking, behavior, or mood; you may:

- Become irritable and intolerant of even minor disturbances;
- Feel irritated or frustrated, lose your temper more often, and yell at others for no reason;
- Feel jumpy or exhausted all the time;
- Find it hard to concentrate or focus on tasks;
- Worry too much about insignificant things;
- Doubt your ability to do things;
- Imagine negative, worrisome, or terrifying scenes;
- Feel you are missing opportunities because you cannot act quickly enough.[9]

---

8 Note — these are the things that have worked for me — they may not be right for you. That's the beauty — we get to choose what is right for us — we get to create new solutions and new paradigms. Just because we are used to doing things one way, doesn't mean we have to do them this way for ever.

9 Source: http://www.webmd.com/balance/stress-management/stress-management-effects-of-stress

Long-term stress also has implications for the immune system, cardiovascular disease and other health-related issues.[10]

As on an airplane when the announcement comes on about what to do if the oxygen is cut off and you have to first help yourself in order to serve others — so it is with balance and our lives. First, we have to see the value of and learn how to care for ourselves, so we have the capacity to be of service to clients, peers and others.

Balance is a Lifelong Practice

There may be some weeks when we are happier with our progress than others. So, relax into it — we're in it for the long term. Also, the context of our life changes along with our priorities so balance will need to be flexible and adjustable. Once we see a new possibility for how to think about balance, clarify what our values are and what is important to us, we can develop new awareness about ourselves and the beliefs that might be limiting us. We can make different choices about what we let into our life and what we let go of, and we can *practice* new habits around balance.

Sometimes we make stakes so high that we become paralyzed and can't seem to find a way forward or see a different possibility. It can be this way with balance. Leaders may believe that they can either have it or they can't, it's all or nothing. They can either have a personal life including a family or they can have a successful career, but not both.

When we become locked into one way of thinking we can become rigid in our perspective, and this can create stress and worry. What can be helpful is to learn flexibility of thinking and self-awareness of when we are stuck. We can develop the competency to self-manage — to notice when we are stuck and step back and say to ourselves, *Oh yes, I'm stuck — how can I get out of this?*

We remember to consider there may be other possibilities, those we may not yet be aware of. Maybe it will take talking to a friend, finding a mentor who has been through this before, or hiring a coach — whatever it takes to get unstuck from the *there's only one way to think about this mode of thinking*.

We can make the choice to try out some different things, baby steps that help us feel confident and that aren't overwhelming. Often this means letting go of one thing that can wait until tomorrow or next week; so that we create space to rest and step out of the frantic pace we are used to. Just getting back a bit of control over our busy lives and begin building the muscle of *actively practicing balance* will make all the difference when you are feeling overwhelmed.

Balance is a Learning to Live Authentically in Each Part of our Life

The benefits of work-life balance:
- It supports us to be more effective leaders as we are able to live from integrity as we become authentic in all parts of our lives;
- It helps us to relax and minimize the distractions of stress which is key to tapping into our free-flow mode of thinking or our intuition;
- It supports us to be more productive as we have a clear mind more of the time — particularly when we need to navigate through new territory where creativity and original thought is needed. It also provides more choice in how we respond to situations as they arise.

---

10 Ibid.

It can mean improved quality of productivity and relationships as leaders are able to keep perspective in times of turmoil. Have you ever noticed the inefficiencies — some call it spin — that occurs with team members who are under continuous stress? Work-life balance supports a focus on immediate priorities as situations in other parts of our lives are managed in a way true to who we are. We can minimize the time that we would normally spend worrying.

And finally, the practice of constantly navigating trade-offs between personal life and work (as well as developing new, mutually beneficial solutions) can be seen as a microcosm for developing the competency for creating new paradigms in business and in organizations that leaders are being called to develop in the world today.

Developing new paradigms requires creativity and original thought; creativity requires relaxation into free-flow thinking, and work-life balance is foundational to this.

Cultivating Just a Little Bit More Work-life Balance

I'll outline the full process, with the caveat that I recommend starting small and keeping it simple. Baby steps are required so an already overwhelming life doesn't get any more so. It's like when a bathtub is overflowing and what we need to do first is turn off the tap to stop any more water coming in. Then we need to empty out a bit so it doesn't feel quite so full. Finally, we can get a feel for where we are and make adjustments to the temperature.

The process for achieving work-life balance:

- Make space in your life for development — learning to practice work-life balance is development and takes some effort;
- Spend some time reflecting on what old beliefs might be getting in the way; for example, that *self-care is frivolous* or that *slowing down is unproductive*. This provides the opportunity to recognize how you deal with stress — or don't deal with it, and then open to new ways of thinking that can be uncomfortable at times;
- Clarify your values and what is really important in your life;
- Clarify the values of your organization as well as the realities and needs of the business;
- Explore possibilities that respect yourself and the needs of the business when your life feels out of balance;
- Learn to slow and make peace with your racing mind;
- Develop new awareness, habits and foundational practices;
- Use each day and week as an opportunity to practice living in a way that feels balanced.

Start small and keep it simple. When we are out of balance, we may have been this way for a while and any changes may seem overwhelming.

ACTION STEPS

Reflections

How do you think about balance — what does it mean to you?

What is your level of self-awareness about balance? What are your automatic patterns regarding balance? Your patterns when you feel well include the following: For example, quit work before dinner, have a cup of herbal tea before bed, go for a walk with my partner/significant other, have a good sleep, go to the gym to begin my day…

Your patterns when you're less healthy include the following: For example, working late, not getting enough sleep, having too much caffeine, eating lots of junk food...

What old beliefs or habits may need to shift in order to have just a little more balance in your life? For example, all or nothing mindset — *I can either have balance or I can't…forever.* It may be helpful for this to shift to I will have balance more of the time and at times, I will be out of balance as life changes. *I'm in it for the long term, so I'll give myself a break and get back to my practices as soon as I become aware that I am out of balance.*

AWAKEN YOUR AUTHENTIC LEADERSHIP – AUTHENTIC LEADERSHIP CONVERSATIONS

What are your values and how can they support you in having more balance?

What are three to five words that describe your core values? How do you know? For example, integrity, family/relationships, wellness, success, sustainability, adventure.

How can my values guide me in making tradeoffs in order to have more balance in my life? For example, *If I value wellness and family, then working eighty hours a week may need to shift for me to have more balance.*

Exercise

Using the instructions and example below, complete the following work-life balance diagram to get a sense of your current state of balance:

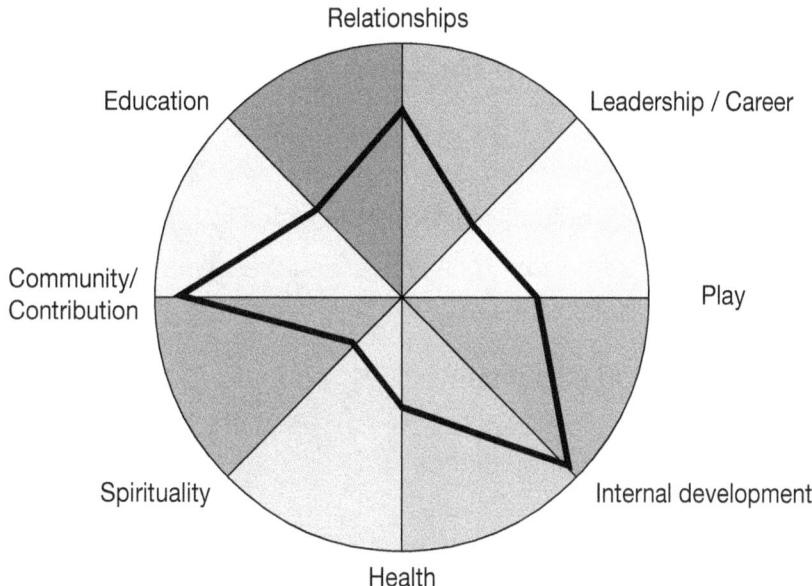

Diagram One — example of one person's current work-life balance

In a simple way, this diagram shows what the different parts of this person's life include and the amount of effort/energy they are spending in each of them. The outside of the circle is the optimal level and the line shows the current levels for each part.

It gives an indication about which areas she/he may be feeling out of balance and may want to make adjustments in. In the example, this person is happy with the level of energy/time he/she spends on community and contribution, relationships and internal development. One area she/he would like to focus on is health.

Instructions for completing your work-life balance diagram:

- Identify and name the different parts of your life — relationships, career, contribution, abundance — use your own words/labels for what is meaningful for you;
- Assume the outer edge of the circle is your optimal amount within that component in your life. For example, you want to add some education in your life through continuing education at your community college, but you don't want to pursue a PhD. Assume the center of the circle is a zero and the outer edge is a ten. This provides a simple way of showing the relative importance of each component to you;
- Place a dot on the line for each component to show where you are currently. For example, in the diagram above it shows community / contribution as about an eight out of ten. This means that the person has quite a lot of this relative to, let's say, health in their life currently. When they assess their whole life, they may want to make adjustments to focus more on health. Or maybe not. The system is designed to be flexible and to fit each person's life and language. There are no judgments attached (that one is better than another — just that this is merely the current state);

- Once you have a dot on each line, join them with a line to show the relative balance in your life currently;
- Reflect on what this tells you as you become more self-aware. Think about what adjustments you might want to make in your life to, if any, to shift the balance to one you are comfortable with in the context of your life currently.

My Current Verses Optimal Life Balance

Reflections

Decide on one area of your life you'd like to adjust in order to have more balance

Given your values and your current balance, one area of your life where you would like to adjust your balance would be _____. For example, *Play*

Consider the realities of making adjustments:

- What are the realities, family and business, and needs that you need to consider and respect when looking at possibilities for trade-offs?

- How could you think through all the possible solutions? Who could support you? For example, *We have a large project coming up where I'll have to work weekends for the next two weeks — I'll need to check with my peers/boss in case this may go longer.*

- What will the trade-offs be if you make adjustments, and how can your values help you decide the right way to make the adjustment? For example, *For the next two weeks I may need to ask my parents to support my partner and I by taking our child for one day a weekend; I'll book a long weekend away with my family once the project is over.*

CREATING WORK-LIFE BALANCE

- What might be challenging in making changes to have more balance? For example, *I may not be used to asking my boss for a day off for the long weekend I want to book; I may not be used to asking my parents or friends for help.*

- What support might you need? Who could you ask to support me?

- What conversations do you need to have?

Building the skills and confidence for having difficult conversations is one of the most important skills for practicing work-life balance. They may be needed in order to navigate through new situations and to brainstorm new possibilities.

Practices

Making space and energy for change towards balance

For the next three months, each week, remove one thing from your *to-do* list and replace it with fifteen-thirty minutes of something that is just for you. For example, take a bath and listen to your favorite music, meditate, go for a walk and notice the flowers, journal when you first wake up. Notice how it feels to take time for you and notice what thoughts come up for you.

Reconfiguring your week to be rejuvenated on Friday afternoon:

- For the next month, each Monday morning for ten minutes, review your schedule and consider what adjustments might be required in order for there to be *just a little more balance*. Make the adjustments to your calendar;
- On Friday, reflect on what you have learned;
- Notice your energy levels on Friday afternoon;
- What will you do differently in the next week as a result of what you have learned?

My simple plan – keep it simple so it's more realistic – for beginning to practice balance in my life. Example:

The Area of life I need more balance in; The Benefit:
More time for rest (as work consists of back to back meetings and we have 2 kids). **Benefit:** I'll be more effective as a boss and a parent as I feel less resentful.
The Belief I need to shift towards:
That time to care for myself is important and I value myself enough to book the time and keep the promise to myself.
The Action I need to commit to:
Book one and a half hours a week to go for a walk in the forest on my own or go for coffee, or to the spa, etc.
The Support I will need:
Someone to take the kids so I can keep my commitment to myself.
The Conversations I will need to have:
Ask my wife/partner to support me when I want to let go of this promise to myself. Ask my wife/partner how I can support her in booking time for herself as well.

CREATING WORK-LIFE BALANCE

The Area of life I need more balance in; The Benefit:
The Belief I need to shift towards:
The Action I need to commit to:
The Support I will need:
The Conversations I will need to have:

Arc of Intense Energy Reflection

Refer to the diagram and description of the Arc of Intense Energy on page 17. Reflect on the topic of this chapter — creating work-life balance. Answer the following questions in order to understand how the arc is showing up for you:

What is your old, automatic pattern when triggered? For example, *When I am triggered by yet another request for my overbooked schedule, I accept and then feel stressed and frustrated.*

What is a new behaviour, belief or attitude you would like to choose instead? For example, *When I am triggered by yet another request for my overbooked schedule, notice the feelings of stress and frustration; and I pause before I accept to evaluate the request in the context of my week; I may or may not accept.*

Practice self-managing through the arc when you are learning about this topic. Begin by paying attention; noticing the energy or discomfort intensifying in the body. As this occurs, practice relaxing your shoulders and belly and deepen and slow your breathing.

This will allow you to feel the emotions as they arise, notice your thoughts and discern if they are aligned with your values or just old, unhelpful messages.

When you learn to discern which is true and right, you will be able to maintain your perspective and choose a response that is appropriate, and authentic, for the situation at hand.

Remember your responses to these two questions. Practice using the new behaviour, belief or attitude as your response when triggered.

After a few weeks of practicing, reflect on what you are learning and how you will adjust your thoughts and behaviours as a result.

Closing Reading

*When we slow down to the speed of life, we tap into a peaceful feeling that
Permeates our entire being and way of life.*

*Rather than constantly feeling rushed, hurried, and frustrated,
we feel calm, joyful and curious...*

*We have many of the same issues to contend with, but they look different.
Rather than appearing to be emergencies that are smothering us, they look like (manageable)
issues that need resolving or opportunities in disguise*[11]

---

[11] Richard Carlson and Joseph Bailey, Slowing Down the Speed of Life — How to Create a More Peaceful, simpler life from the inside out, P 54, 1997.

Effective communication skills were elusive to me when I began my career and I shut down when confronted with an overly aggressive counterpart. It hampered my leadership and caused levels of stress, sometimes for years, that was not necessary once I began to learn how to have them.

In every team and in every organization, I recognized that this one topic was an opportunity for improvement for authenticity. If a leader learned how to convey their message more effectively in an uncomfortable situation or under intense stress, they could stay true to themselves and the impact on themselves and others were much more positive… even when the message was a very difficult one.

I wrote the original worksheet from my perspective as someone who was intimidated by others and had to learn to stand up for myself to speak my truth. I quickly realized that there were also times when I intimated others who felt a power imbalance with me as their leader. I experienced colleagues and clients who, intentionally and knowingly, used intimidation and fear as a way to manage others. I believe they thought it would improve their employees' performance. All the while, this behaviour had a negative impact on the self-esteem and productivity of their team.

I have worried a lot about the shock-absorber level of the organization — the layer of leaders reporting to a tyrant who left a path of destruction in her/his wake. Learning to stand up for yourself is one antidote to this kind of a leader. Leaving the situation is another.

This topic continues to be the second most popular one, next to managing the inner critic.

Having Difficult Conversations

— Action Worksheet —

Topic Description:
How can I say anything when I feel intimidated?

How do I stay centered and clear during a difficult conversation when I feel intimidated by someone or when I am perceived as intimidating to others?

Use the following worksheet for developing your ability to have difficult conversations when you feel intimidated by another person, or if you are the one perceived to be intimidating to others. While it is written from the perspective of a person who is intimidated by others, it can be adapted for leaders who are perceived as intimidating.

Feel free to make a copy of this worksheet so you can use it over and over again. Remember that having the actual conversation is about thirty percent of the steps required — there are things you can do to support yourself before, during, and after the conversation.

A caveat about difficult conversations is that the best way to have them is face-to-face, next is via phone or video technology. Email or text are to be avoided for these kinds of interactions as the receiver may misinterpret the message and the sender may use it to avoid having the difficult conversation.

Another caveat is that there may be a power differential with the person you are having the conversation with. Remember that good leaders surround themselves with people who give them feedback, particularly when a course correction is required. It is essential to create the right environment for the person on the receiving end to feel safe so the message can be heard.

Remember that you will return to a beginner's mind as you learn a new skill. Compassion for yourself when you may stumble and seeing each time you practice as progress is essential for continuous learning.

Things to Consider When Thinking About Having Difficult Conversations

Difficult Conversations Are:
- *Gifts* we are given over and over again in our lives and building capacity for them can help us manage stress and minimize suffering;
- Confidence-building opportunities;
- Opportunities to develop the skills to engage in them;
- Less difficult over time with support and practice.

Difficult Conversations are *gifts* we are given over and over again

This is one thing in this life we can count on — there will always be times when we are invited to engage in a difficult conversation. We have a choice — we can choose to avoid them which was a strategy I employed for a long time. When I was in a situation where I felt *thrown*, where I felt scared, intimidated or unprepared, I employed my preferred *defense mechanism* of the day in order to cope. I cried, got confused, forgot what I wanted to say, or my favorite — shut down and withdrew. At the time, I had no idea this was what I was doing.

I had no idea how this impacted my confidence either. When I withdrew, I lost my confidence around that person. I assumed the next interaction would go the same way and, in a way, I created the conditions for it to go badly.

I went to feeling intimidated and therefore act a certain way. I played a role in the dynamic that I never realized until I began developing self-awareness about my automatic patterns. A coach who supported me at the time asked me what my role in the dynamic was. I blamed it all on the other person and initially took no responsibility for my part in it. It was all *her fault* that I felt intimidated when a big part of it was actually my issue — I felt intimidated and I thought and behaved accordingly — that was what I needed to explore.

Instead of withdrawing and shutting down, we can learn to stay centered, to stay engaged, and build our capacity and competency within the process. After several years of practice and support, the kind of conversation wherein I feel intimidated and the kind of body language and intensity on the part of the other person is much less of an issue for me. I have built my capacity for staying centered — I can observe what is happening for me in the moment and can say to myself, *ah yes, this is interesting — I'm noticing that I am making an assumption, I am starting to feel stressed*. I can then I let it go, stay in the conversation, and stay present which means that the assumptions take a back seat. I am so grateful for this more mature approach.

I am now used to and understand that there are different kinds of people; we all have different personalities, and that is wonderful. While I like calm and deep conversation, others like lively and loud debate, in fact, some love it. In the past, my frame of reference for what was intimidating was different — it was based on fear. Now, I go with the flow more and enjoy the debate once I listen to my opinion. And where there is an issue of bullying and intentional intimidation, I protect myself and speak my truth and/or leave a situation that is unhealthy for me. I can now experience these conversations and let them go rather than obsess over them, what sometimes used to be for months and even years. These situations have much less charge for me than they used to — bring them on, I can handle them!

Each Difficult Conversation can be a confidence-building opportunity

We experience different situations — sometimes we have to respond in the moment and sometimes we have the luxury of time to prepare. I'd like to share two examples with you. First, I'll provide context and then I will share what I did to navigate each.

- With a boss where the relationship was important to me;
- With a peer when we had to work together and we experienced tension over a number of years.

With a boss where the relationship was important to me:

I noticed that we developed an unhelpful pattern within our interactions — if I was having a good day and she was having a good day, we interacted well. If, however, I was having a low self-esteem day or if she was having a day where she was angry at something or distracted and not present, we had difficult interactions. I noticed her body language — her voice got louder, her eyes opened wider, and she sat forward at the table. It felt aggressive and I felt intimidated.

I experienced confusion and my throat became dry, I was unable to stay clear and I rambled. She then got more frustrated (my assumption) and I got more scattered. I got out of her office as quickly as possible.

I obsessed and worried about the interaction and felt that she didn't like me anymore. I lost my confidence and when I went back in the next day or week thinking it would happen again — it did. Even if I had a good day and was completely prepared and she had a bad day, I took on her mood and the interaction would go badly. And the cycle continued.

With a peer where we had experienced tension for years:

There was one person I worked with who triggered me within our relationship and I had no idea about the dynamic of it. In my mind, it was all her fault. Ironically, I received coaching support from her for three years in a row. I was the visionary starter in the corporate group who came up with the great ideas for how to make things better — how to improve processes around implementing strategy. She was the person in operations in one of the business units, the implementer. She was constantly angry with my ideas and shot them down always seeing the risks and flaws in them. I hated it. She was constantly raining on my parade. The project we worked on together was three and a half years long and we were just beginning.

We can learn how and build skills

We may not know how to have these kinds of conversations. This was quite a revelation for me when I learned I could develop actual skills to support me. Some of these include learning how to prepare for them:

- Deciding on what I wanted to say and how I would say it;
- Reflecting on my physical presence — remembering to breathe and think about how I would sit;
- Thinking about what I would do if I felt the conversation was at a standstill or if the person began to yell;
- Choosing to debrief and celebrate what I learned;
- Learning about judgments and assumptions I was making that got in my way of connecting with the other person;
- Being mindful of letting my walls down and speaking my truth — saying what I knew to be true and inquire from a place of curiosity verses defensiveness;
- Discovering how I could learn about compassion for myself; I felt I was in the kindergarten class of how to have a difficult conversation when I was actually a senior manager and a business owner.

Again, over time and with lots of support and practice, I changed how I see these situations — from something I needed to avoid at all costs to gifts I was given providing the next opportunity for my development. They will always be there just like the person I can't get along with at the office. There will always be one in a different body and with a different name. I can reframe how I see each one as my gift to learn about myself, about compassion, and about how I can choose to show up — or not. My personal goal is to make the right choice, not necessarily the easy one.

Less Difficult with Support and Practice

I wish this was part of my education at some point — we never learned how to communicate effectively in school or university — particularly how to have a difficult conversation. I was in Toastmasters for three years and I can't remember the topic ever coming up.

So, I learned some skills on my own, I found some in books, and I received some from trusted family and friends to help me prepare. To move through some difficult conversations, I needed the support of a coach or therapist. It was a wonderful investment and I am so grateful for my path of development. One thing to remember is that it takes time and practice — over and over and over again — in order to be good at something. In a way we are beginners in this area and that's a hard place for high achievers to find themselves in.

Examples of What I Did

With a boss where the relationship was important to me:

I set up a meeting and let her know that I wanted to talk to her about our relationship and that I'd noticed a pattern that I felt we were in and wasn't sure if it was helping us. I was shaking when I went in. I let her know that this relationship was important to me and that I was frustrated by the dynamics I was experiencing. She was open and curious.

I let her know specifically what I experienced in the last few interactions. I let her know what I was experiencing in terms of how I felt and what I experienced from her tone and body language. I asked her to share with me what her experience was.

It turned out that she had some unresolved anger with me about something that happened in the past. I noticed a change in both our behavior after it had happened and yet I never put it on the table. We had a good conversation about it and cleared the air. We both reflected on what our role was in letting the relationship change. Within our interactions after this she was more aware of her mood, body language, and tone. I was more aware of not taking it personally, and of checking in rather than making assumptions.

This conversation was a turning point in strengthening our relationship.

With a peer where we had experienced tension for years:

I actually worked on this situation over a series of years and within many interactions. I began by learning about both our personality styles with an emphasis on my automatic patterns. I reflected on what I knew about her — she was analytical and liked statistics and proof. She also liked to get to the point and to minimize small talk. She liked to go to action as well and to have solutions be grounded in reality and to provide a pragmatic and useful approach.

Regarding myself, I learned that what I perceived as aggressive, others viewed as just a louder tone of voice. I learned that when I became stressed, I held tension in my shoulders, my breath became shallow and I got clammy, cold hands. I got confused and wanted to cry (sometimes I would), then I shut down and withdrew.

What I learned to do was match her energy — to stay in the debate. I watched my body language and I sat with strength, made full eye contact and focused on deepening my breathing. I remember one particular interaction where I stayed strong in what I thought was the right way to proceed. I didn't back down this time and it proved to be a good move for the company. She agreed.

This relationship stayed the same over the years with an ability to work together without a lot of warmth. What shifted for me when we met was my ability to take care of myself and come back to center over and over again and to experience how her approach and personality had less of a trigger for me. I was also able to shift how I saw her and respected how her pragmatic approach actually grounded my visionary approach. The outcomes were better as a result of us working together.

ACTION STEPS

Practices

Practice takes place on several levels. On a somatic level it includes learning to relax into deep belly breathing — quite the contrary to what I learned as a child. *Suck in your tummy* was a phrase I remember learning in ballet when I was five and one stuck with me until I was forty-three and re-learned how to relax my belly, take deep breaths, and stay present in the moment. This seemingly simple practice has been a savior to me within my journey to build capacity to have difficult conversations. It allows me to step back for a moment, re-center and be choice-ful about how I would respond — to become clear about what I will say next.

Next, practice means building new habits such as jotting down a few notes about my thoughts in the moment or declaring that I need a minute to regroup before proceeding. In the book *Crucial Conversations*, the authors, Joseph Grenny, Al Switzler, and Ron McMillan, talk about stepping out of a conversation any time you feel unsafe in order to reestablish a comfortable environment before proceeding and they provide several ways to do this. Practice can include preparing my thoughts, role playing with someone, person A, who will support me, then proceeding with the conversation with another, person B, and then debriefing with the supportive person A after it is complete.

Each time I encounter a situation where I know it will be difficult for me to speak my truth I remember how it felt the last time I entered into one and made it through — even if I may have only said half of what I wanted to say. that little glint of self-confidence I experienced as a result stayed with me. The fact that I was able to stay in the conversation despite my dry throat, sweaty palms, and desire to turn and run out of the room was an accomplishment, a baby step. And with each baby step, the progress is cumulative.

I remember thinking, *Maybe I can do this. Just maybe I am getting stronger as a leader*. This was powerful for me. It gave me the confidence knowing that I could handle the next one, and the next.

When developing the competence for having a difficult conversation, it can be helpful to first practice when you have time to prepare. This gives you a foundation for the future when you need to have one in the moment.

Steps to Support You Before, During, and After a Difficult Conversation

Before the conversation

Reflect on and answer the following questions regarding how you currently deal with difficult conversations. Again, this worksheet is written from the perspective when the person having the conversation feels intimidated by the person they need to have it with. If you are in the opposite position, where you are perceived to be intimidating, reflect on each question from your perspective.

- How do you think about difficult conversations? Are they something you are used to engaging in? Or, are they to be avoided at all costs?

- Write down what your automatic patterns and beliefs are for having difficult conversations. When you begin to work on difficult conversations you may not even be aware of your automatic patterns.

- Use the following reflections for one month to begin to develop your awareness:
    - Reflect at the end of each week in your journal or on a sheet of paper for ten minutes about situations when you felt intimidated by others.
    - Ask yourself the following: What was it about the specific situation that you were uncomfortable with? What was it about the other person that you felt intimidated by?
    - What pattern did you use in this situation to help you cope? How did you feel in the moment? What did you experience in my body?
    - Reflect on what you are learning about yourself in each situation and what you can do differently as a result?

HAVING DIFFICULT CONVERSATIONS

- If you aren't aware of yours it can be helpful to ask others, friends, family, peers, etc., what they believe yours are.
    - Your automatic patterns for having difficult conversations are:

    - Your beliefs about having difficult conversations are:

- Prepare your thoughts both for what your objective is for the conversation, for what occurred that caused you to want to have the difficult conversation. Then, clarify what you can do differently that would be helpful. Use a specific example of something you experienced rather than hearsay.
For example, *I sent you an email and followed up with a phone call about something I needed to get done by yesterday for our supervisor. I never heard back from you. I wanted to check out what happened.*
    - Your objective for this conversation is:

- What you want to have the conversation about; this is the specific thing you experienced that felt uncomfortable for you:

- Be clear about what it is that you would like from the person if it happens again:
  For example, *what would be helpful for me is, if you disagree with the approach or don't have time to respond, you call me and we talk about it before the deadline is up.* What would be helpful in the future is:

- Role play to practice prior to having the conversation. It can be helpful to find an appropriate person who you trust, who is not involved, who will keep it confidential, and who can provide you with support and feedback on your proposed approach — someone who has the courage to tell you how you come across and will provide the feedback in a respectful way. Role play the situation and reflect on learnings. Adjust your approach as required. Bring your notes with you to the meeting with the person.
- When you are ready to have the conversation set up a time and location with the person and let them know what you'd like to talk about:
  For example, you want to check in about something that happened yesterday and it will take about fifteen minutes. Use the space below to write the time, location, and contact information down. If you talk to them without setting up a time in advance, ask them if now is a good time for them to talk. If not, set up a time that works for both of you. Think about the location — somewhere private where you won't be interrupted.

Time:

Location:

Phone number if not face to face or online technology contact information:

- If you have foundational practices, these are the days when they are most important to keep in place. While they may seem simple, they are actually essential and will support you to have more capacity for these kinds of conversations:
    - Get enough sleep;
    - Ensure your nutrition supports you, including lots of water;
    - Exercise and meditate to calm the nervous system;
    - Any other practices you have in place like journaling, etc.

Write down the foundational practices you have in place or will need to put in place the day before and day of the conversation. The foundational practices that will support me to have the conversation are:

During the conversation

- Using your notes if needed while having the conversation.
    - First, share what you'd like to talk to the person about and check in with them about their experience of it. You can let them know that this is difficult for you if you feel it is appropriate.
    Be specific about what occurred and how you felt as a result.
    - Listen with a willingness to be influenced as old beliefs and assumptions may distort the experience for us. Other influencers can be how tired we are on the day it occurred, how stressed we are, how distracted we are, how present we are. Ask her/him to say more about what his/her experience was so you deepen your understanding of them. This will give you a moment to regain your composure and stay present in the conversation even if you are nervous. For example, you can ask, *Can you say more about that?*
    - Confirm what you have agreed upon and what the next steps are. Thank him/her for having the conversation with you.

Note: There is an *Arc* of Intense Energy and emotions that builds and then dissipates over time and when you are in the middle of the conversation. It is at the most intense point when you may feel so uncomfortable that you revert to your automatic pattern. As you develop capacity for staying present in increasingly intense situations you will be able to choose your response rather than going to your *autopilot*. With practice, the intensity of the Arc is diminished and your confidence will improve.

- The importance of breathing. if you find yourself getting nervous and your mouth gets dry, practice deep belly breathing. It may sound strange but it works! Often when you are stressed, your body goes into the *fight or flight* response. You tighten your stomach, your breathing becomes shallow, and you hunch up your shoulders. By relaxing and breathing through this, you support yourself in staying clear-headed when you are stressed. Right down the word *breathe* in your notes to remind you to keep breathing as you continue the conversation. Notice this as you are within the conversation in order to distract your mind from the fight or flight response that fear evokes.

After the conversation

- Developing your competency for emotional intelligence and the ability to stay authentic in difficult situations requires continuous learning. What can be helpful is practicing debriefs and reflection in order to clarify your learnings and adjust your approach for the next time.
  Debrief: either meet with the person who supported you in the role play or reflect on the situation and answer the following questions on your own:

    - What is one thing you can do differently next time as a result of what you learned?

    - What two things did you do well? Remember that your inner critic will want to focus on the negative. It can be helpful to balance this out with two things you did well — think of these as progress:

  By seeing difficult conversations as opportunities to learn, you can more readily accept them as they come up. You will grow in your leadership, as well as, support other employees as you do.

Arc of Intense Energy Reflection

Refer to the diagram and description of the Arc of Intense Energy on page 17. Reflect on the topic of this chapter — having difficult conversations. Answer the following questions in order to understand how the arc is showing up for you:

What is your old, automatic pattern when triggered? For example, *When I am triggered by a situation where I strongly disagree with how I have been treated, I say nothing and then notice my feeling of resentment and I avoid the person.*

What is a new behaviour, belief or attitude you would like to choose instead? For example, *When I am triggered by a situation where I strongly disagree with how I have been treated, I notice my feelings of resentment and set up time to speak in private and respectfully call the person on their behaviour.*

Practice self-managing through the arc when you are learning about this topic. Begin by paying attention; noticing the energy or discomfort intensifying in the body. As this occurs, practice relaxing your shoulders and belly and deepen and slow your breathing.

This will allow you to feel the emotions as they arise, notice your thoughts and discern if they are aligned with your values or just old, unhelpful messages.

When you learn to discern which is true and right, you will be able to maintain your perspective and choose a response that is appropriate, and authentic, for the situation at hand.

Remember your responses to these two questions. Practice using the new behaviour, belief or attitude as your response when triggered.

After a few weeks of practicing, reflect on what you are learning and how you will adjust your thoughts and behaviours as a result.

Closing Reading

Out beyond ideas of wrong doing and right doing there is a field. I'll meet you there.[12]

---

[12] Sufi poet Rumi, as quoted by Marshall B. Rosenberg, Ph.D. in "Nonviolent Communication — A Language of Life" 2nd Edition, p 15, 2005.

> I had a great awakening when I read the book, *The Dance of Anger* by Harriet Lerner. I learned that, as a leader, I was both an over-*functioner* and an under-*functioner* in different situations. I will never forget when a very senior leader who was new to working for me said, *You know, there are a few things you are working on that I really can take over* — this was his very kind way of letting me know that I was micromanaging him. I was in a new role on an executive leadership team and I was not yet confident in this new environment. So, I went back to what I knew which was how to do his job.
>
> In another situation I relied on others to do the bulk of the work as my lack of confidence got in the way of pulling my weight and contributing equally to the task.
>
> With a high level of empathy, I found myself overwhelmed and wanting to control and caretake and saw this in other leaders as well. I learned that the antidote was to sit quietly while building capacity to be with the discomfort of not immediately saying yes and putting my hand up for the next project or opportunity — to take the time to evaluate the request within the context of my overly full plate and to finally say, *no*.
>
> Inevitably there was someone who stepped forward to take on the task. I learned to be my authentic self by noticing my ego as it didn't like the fact that someone else was getting the recognition. By letting the thoughts go, I could realize the positive progress by saying no and leaving space for my life.

Saying No and Setting Boundaries

— Action Worksheet —

> **Topic Description:**
> *I just can't take that on!*
> *How do I learn to say No and feel ok with it?*

Can you think of a time when you said yes to a task or situation, but you really wanted to say no? What was it like for you? What was the impact it had?

Over the course of our life, we may receive the message that we are the helpers in the world. We are the ones who need to take things on and make them better. Sometimes, we get the message that if we don't say, yes, we should feel guilty and that it just won't be right. This can become our pattern to receiving self-esteem from external sources rather than from within.

Do any of these situations sound familiar? Are you the manager who continues to *do* rather than delegate to her team member? *It's too much effort to explain all the details, so I'll just do that myself.* Or, the executive who takes on more groups and accountabilities rather than being thoughtful about how much will be too much for him. *Of course, I can take on that new group with thirty extra people. How will I manage? I'll figure it out.* You might even be that man who books events every night of the week — volunteering, going to school, social events for work — and then crashes on the weekend.

Or, are you the woman who does everything around the house rather than having a conversation about splitting up the duties and asking for what she needs? *I can do it all*, you say to yourself, and then feel resentful toward your partner. You think, *He should know I need help*.

Use the following worksheet to begin practicing learning how to say *no*, where appropriate, in order to support your leadership and your life. Remember that when something is challenging you at work or at home, it will show up in your life in different ways until you wake up to it and make a shift in how you think about it — and then change your habits and behaviours.

Things to Consider When Learning How to Say *No:*

- It can help to understand the interplay between *over-functioning* and anger;
- Slowing and listening to our bodies, our emotions, and feelings can support us in knowing when we are taking on too much;
- Clarifying what is acceptable to us — our values and boundaries — and building the skill of having difficult conversations is the next step in saying no;
- Compassion is key as we learn a new way; we're in this for the long term and progress isn't linear.

In addition, practicing and noticing how it feels is the way forward, and debriefing for continuous learning is important for any new skill we are building.

Over-functioning[13] and anger

Some leaders receive self-esteem by getting people to like them so they feel valued. We may believe that if we do things for others, they will like us and conversely, if we say *no*, they will stop liking us. And so, we adopt a pattern, a habit of over-functioning. We continue to say *yes* to this project and that project and whatever else comes our way when it may or may not be in line with our accountabilities at work or with what we love in life in general.

We're just used to saying yes.

When we give and give of ourselves until the other person or people can't possibly give the same amount, we can become resentful that they aren't giving at the same level as us. In our minds, they under-function even when giving at that level wouldn't be appropriate anyway. We don't always tell them what we want or what is too much for us, and yet we expect them to just know and do as much as us. We may become annoyed with them as they set the boundaries that we are unable to. And if we aren't able to feel our anger, we simply push it down which may work for a while, but it comes back in one way or another.

For example, two team members work on a series of projects together. One person consistently takes on more work than the other — they need to be in control, and they want to be liked. This person may be resentful of the other person who practices work-life balance differently and who sets boundaries when the workload gets too heavy. The first person continues to over-function, gets resentful, and can't understand why the other person won't work just as hard.

Slowing and listening to our body, emotions, and feelings

Some leaders have a hard time feeling their emotions, particularly anger. This is why learning to listen to the signals our bodies give us is so important.

What is it like for you when sitting in a meeting and someone asks for a volunteer, and then they wait? What do you feel when this happens? Do you contract and hunch your shoulders? Do you immediately say yes?

If so, it may be because you're experiencing the discomfort of the silence while waiting for someone else to volunteer. So, you volunteer in order to dissipate your own discomfort of the feelings you have a hard time sitting with even when you already have way too much on your plate as it is. Then you get angry.

Learning how to both feel and express anger can support leaders to practice how to say no. Many people have a very hard time actually feeling anger and some never do. They push it down into their subconscious and it manifests in one way or another. Passive aggressive behaviour is one way it may show up. Talking behind someone's back to build coalitions of support is another.

Quite often, once we learn to feel our anger, the flood gates we expected to open end up just being emotions and thoughts that last a short time and then go away. A new spaciousness opens up as we feel and release these emotions. Anger is healthy and important for us to listen to and respond from.

It is also important in general to relax so that we can experience the sensations and feelings in different situations. An anxiousness in the pit of your stomach can mean your intuition is giving you a signal. Once you learn to experience this and interpret it, you are given additional information for navigating all sorts of situations.

---

[13] Harriet Lerner, Ph.D., The Dance of Anger — A Woman's Guide to Changing the Patterns of Intimate Relationships, Note, while this book focuses on these patterns for women, the principles apply to both men and women.

Clarifying what is acceptable to us

We can learn how to use our values to set boundaries. Values are deeply held beliefs about what is important to us and how we want to live. They are, essentially, your *bottom line*. Spend some time articulating your values and keep them with you. Share your values with others and have a conversation about them. This will help to deepen your understanding and commitment to them and check them against other possible values to ensure these are the most important ones for you.

Your values support you to make decisions and set boundaries. Boundaries are a way of defining what is acceptable to us and what is not.

Sometimes we don't know what our boundaries are. If we are not able to feel our emotions and what is going on in our bodies, we may just experience the situation as something that isn't working for us or something that feels weird and we just can't explain. When we begin to feel them, we become aware of signals that can support us in knowing when it's time to say no when we may have automatically been following our unconscious habit of saying yes. For example, *I am feeling a tightness in my chest and my breathing is going shallow; when this happens, it means that if I take this on, it will be too much for me.* Or, *I really want tonight off and yet I find myself saying yes to a friend who has given me a last-minute invite to a play and dinner.* Learning how to say no is a way to honour ourselves and practice self-care. When we don't, it feels like we are breaking a promise to ourselves.

As we support ourselves by doing what we really want, we build our self-esteem and our confidence. It's an upward spiral that builds and builds. At the same time, we undo an old habit, one that we can't even remember how long it has been with us.

Compassion for ourselves is the key

Giving ourselves a break can lighten the load and give us the foundational support for going forward.

Remember that building any new skill takes time and can feel uncomfortable at first. We may not always perfect it the way we would like to, but we recognize that we are making progress. As we learn, especially in times of stress, we may go back to the old, known way. When this occurs, be compassionate with yourself, reflect on how it felt and what you might do differently next time. Sometimes we have to re-experience the old way again and again until we are finally *done with it* and ready for a shift to occur. Because there will be a next time, you can count on it. Practice noticing resistance and then overriding it to see it as your gift in life and the next opportunity to learn.

As you build capacity, situations which, in the past, seemed ominous will have less and less impact on you. You'll be able to say *no* in more and more situations as you get used to it, when you are aware of the momentary discomfort that might come as you set a boundary. You do this through what in the past would have been a difficult conversation. It becomes your new way as you shift away from the old.

ACTION STEPS

Reflections

Clarify your awareness about saying no

- How do you think about saying no? In what situations is it easy? And which are difficult?

- What are your automatic patterns and beliefs that might impact when you are able to say *no* and be OK with it?

- Are you an *over-functioner* consistently offering to do more than you are accountable for, or have the capacity to do? Or, are you an *under-functioner* leaving the work you could be a part of completing to others knowing it would be a better product if you were involved, as well as, giving the other person a break? It is important to know the difference between having healthy boundaries around a situation versus *under-functioning*.
For example, two team members work on a series of projects together. One person, Sharon, consistently takes on more work than the other as she needs to be in control and wants to be liked. This person may be resentful of the other person, Joe, who continuously deflects work onto others and doesn't do his part in completing the project. Joe may say he will participate, but then doesn't follow through. Sharon continues to *over-function*, becomes resentful and can't understand why Joe won't work just as hard. The *under-functioner*, Joe, may or may not be conscious of his beliefs and behaviours.

SAYING NO AND SETTING BOUNDARIES

- What beliefs, automatic patterns and habits, if they shifted or changed, would support you in saying *no* going forward?
  For example, *I value myself and am noticing I'm feeling overwhelmed, so I'll cancel the dinner arrangements I made this Friday and stay home and rest instead.*

Slow and listen to your body

Being aware of your emotions and feelings can support you in knowing when you are taking on too much.

- In what situations do you have a problem saying *no*? What is it, specifically, about the situation, that gets in the way?

- What are you experiencing, in my body, during these situations? What are the emotions? What are you thinking? What are you sensing?

Note: There is an *Arc* of intense energy and emotions that build and then dissipate over time when you are in a situation where you may need to say *no*, but feel uncomfortable. It is at the most intense point when you may feel so uncomfortable that you revert to your automatic pattern. As you develop capacity for staying present in increasingly intense situations you will be able to choose your response rather than react using emotions that arise when on autopilot. With practice, the Arc of intense energy diminishes and your confidence improves.

Take the time to breathe

If you find yourself getting nervous and your mouth getting dry, practice deep belly breathing. It may sound strange, but it works! Often, when stressed, your body goes into the fight or flight, or freeze response. You tighten your stomach, your breathing becomes shallow, and you hunch your shoulders. By relaxing and breathing through this, you can support yourself in staying clear-headed. Write the word *breathe* in your notes to remind you to keep breathing as you continue the conversation. Notice this as you are in the conversation in order to distract your mind from the fight or flight response that fear evokes.

Clarify what is acceptable to you by discovering your values and boundaries:

- Use your values as guidance when it is important for you to say *no* in order to honor yourself. Spend some time articulating them and then keep them with you to support you in times of indecisiveness.
List six of your values here:

- Your values support you in making decisions and setting boundaries. Boundaries are a way of defining what is acceptable to you and what is not.
- Ask yourself the following question, *how can my values help me discern if this is right for me at this time?* Use the following simple model to answer this question.

Think of a particular situation at work. Let's say how you want to spend a typical work week. Draw a circle and write all that is acceptable to you if you invite it inside the circle and all that is not outside the circle. For example, inside the circle I write, *what is acceptable to me is working thirty-five–forty hours per week, most of the time*. I also write, *what is acceptable is working on the occasional weekend or evening*. What I write outside of the circle is *What is not acceptable to me is to work every weekend and most evenings*. This makes what the line of your boundary is much clearer. You'll become more decisive about what you want to let into your life and what you may not.

Practices

Learn Self-Compassion

Try the following practices for the next three to six months. Remember it will take the time it needs to take, but not necessarily the time you want it to take when you are making shifts in your beliefs and behaviours. Having self-compassion is the key as you learn a new way.

- **Build awareness:**

    For the next three months, each time you are in a meeting or a situation where they ask for a volunteer to do something, see how long you can sit and not reply. Notice how you feel as you sit and wait. While sitting, ask yourself:

    - What are my values and how can they help me discern if this is right for me at this time?
    - Do I have the time, energy, and resources to do this?
    - What will the impact be on my other work and on my life if I take it on?

    Notice what you are feeling it in your body and reflect on what the signal is telling you.

    Reflect in your journal for 5 minutes about what you learned about yourself and what you can do differently as a result. If your decision is to say yes, notice how it feels and whether it was the right decision for you or not.

- **Practice saying *no*:**

    It helps to take baby steps and practice actually saying the word *no* out loud and in situations that are low-risk. Ask a supportive friend for help over the next few weeks as you practice setting boundaries. When you try this, ask her/him for feedback. Notice how you felt in your body and how that supported you to know when it was time to say *no*. Reflect in your journal on how it felt to take care of yourself by saying no.

- **Debrief:**

    Apply your learnings to the next situation where you need to say *no*. Reflect on the situation and answer the following questions:

    What is one thing you could do differently next time as a result of what you learned?

Focusing on progress and remembering that your inner critic will want to focus on the negative, it can be helpful to balance this out with two things that you did well.

What two things did you do well?

Arc of Intense Energy Reflection

Refer to the diagram and description of the Arc of Intense Energy on page 17. Reflect on the topic of this chapter — saying no and setting boundaries. Answer the following questions in order to understand how the arc is showing up for you:

What is your old, automatic pattern when triggered? For example, *When I am triggered by a situation where I am asked to help with something I really don't want to help with, I notice my discomfort at sitting in silence, quickly say yes to the request and feel angry and resentful.*

What is a new behaviour, belief or attitude you would like to choose instead? For example, *When I am triggered by a situation where I am asked to help with something I really don't want to help with, I notice my discomfort at sitting in silence, I respond with a request to take it away and reflect on it given my other commitments. Or I say No in the moment when I am clear I am not able to help.*

Practice self-managing through the arc when you are learning about this topic. Begin by paying attention; noticing the energy or discomfort intensifying in the body. As this occurs, practice relaxing your shoulders and belly and deepen and slow your breathing.

This will allow you to feel the emotions as they arise, notice your thoughts and discern if they are aligned with your values or just old, unhelpful messages.

When you learn to discern which is true and right, you will be able to maintain your perspective and choose a response that is appropriate, and authentic, for the situation at hand.

Remember your responses to these two questions. Practice using the new behaviour, belief or attitude as your response when triggered.

After a few weeks of practicing, reflect on what you are learning and how you will adjust your thoughts and behaviours as a result.

Closing Reading

For many of us, the most difficult word to say is one of the shortest and easiest in the vocabulary: No.

No — simple to pronounce, hard to say. We're afraid people won't like us, or we feel guilty. We may believe that a so-called good employee, child, parent, spouse never says no.

The problem is, if we don't learn to say no, we stop liking ourselves and the people we always try to please. We may even punish others out of resentment.

When do we say no? When no is what we really mean.

When we learn to say no, people can trust us and we can trust ourselves. All sorts of good things happen when we start saying what we mean.

If we're scared to say no, we can buy some time. We can take a break, rehearse the word, and go back and say no. We don't have to offer long explanations for our decisions.

When we can say no, we can say yes to the good. Our no's and our yes' begin to be taken seriously. We gain control of ourselves.

And we learn a secret, No isn't really that hard to say.[14]

---

14 Adapted from: The Language of Letting Go, Melody Beattie, "Saying No" — August 7th, p 224.

When I became an Integral Coach, I remember having my mind blown open by the Enneagram and its teachings. One of the most profound ideas, though there were many, was that there were three centers of intelligence rather than just the thinking mind.

I remember drawing a picture of myself on one of my first vision boards and, when I looked back on it, realized I only drew a face. The fact that I didn't draw a body and that my body eluded me as I constantly ignored the signals and messages it was giving me on a daily basis, was a completely new awakening.

My body wasn't always a safe place for me and over the years moving through my personal recovery from childhood trauma, I learned to feel emotions and the discomfort of intensely stressful situations, as well as, the joy of incredible happiness. Once I did learn to listen and live with awareness of the three centers, I began to notice that the messages from my intuition and my physical cues informed my thoughts and behaviours and gave me much more to go on when faced with an important decision.

This topic was the most *out there* of all of them when I initially wrote them; I'm so glad that it is much more mainstream now.

Integrating The Three Centers of Intelligence

— Action Worksheet —

> **Topic Description:**
> *I live so much of the time in my head!*
> *How do I integrate the three centers of intelligence to improve my leadership and my life?*

Living each day open to our three centers of intelligence — thinking (head), feeling (heart) and sensing (body) — supports us to be authentic leaders in whatever way we choose to contribute in the world, whether within a non-profit or for-profit organization, as a volunteer, in our personal lives or in the boardroom. The world is calling for role models, people who live day-to-day guided by ethics and strength of character in order to live successful lives while being true to themselves. The world is calling for authentic leadership and women and men are stepping into their authenticity as part of a global movement that is underway.

Use the following worksheet for developing your ability to integrate your three centers of intelligence into your leadership and your life.

One note about this topic:

To practice it is more about learning to *be* than learning to *do*. The focus is on awareness by listening to information we receive through our bodies and our intuition in order to supplement the external information we receive. By being open and aware, we can learn to integrate this information in the moment and choose our responses rather than always accepting our automatic or default patterns of thought. Can you imagine the many ways this would be useful in business?

Things to Consider While Integrating the Three Centers of Intelligence:

- The three centers of intelligence include the heart, head and body;
- Integrating the three centers of intelligence into our leadership makes us more effective and improves the world as we spend time in the creative, free-flow mode of thinking;[15]
- We can learn how to integrate all of these into our leadership and our lives;
- When we do, we experience abundance, wellness, as well as, inner peace more of the time.

The three centers of intelligence

While I grew up learning that the mind was the center of intelligence for the body, over the last few years, I learned that it is not the only one. There are actually three — head, heart, and body.

---

15 Concept of free-flow mode of thinking taken from "Slowing down to the speed of Life — How to Create a more peaceful, simpler life from the inside out", Richard Carlson and Joseph Bailey. Concept of free-flow mode of thinking taken from "Slowing down to the speed of Life — How to Create a more peaceful, simpler life from the inside out", Richard Carlson and Joseph Bailey.

I had no idea I was living ninety percent of my life *in my head* calling it *zoning* or *going off to the next* where I was constantly thinking about the next thing, and the next and the next. I was hardly ever truly present for myself or others. Now when I look back, I see it took an incredible amount of energy for me to live this way as I wasn't being true to myself. I had no idea I could listen to my body for guidance. I did know I had strong intuition and when I listened to it, it was there for me. I didn't always listen to it though.

Most of us in modern societies are almost entirely estranged from the wisdom of our bodies. The psychological term for this is dissociating, in everyday language we call this checking out. In a busy, stress-filled day, it is likely we sense out body only if it is in pain. For instance, we do not usually notice that we have feet unless our shoes are too tight.[16]

Sound familiar?

The good news is there is hope for leaders in this *sped up* world where going fast and *getting things done* is valued sometimes above all else.

Before I talk about how to integrate this into leadership, I want to step back and say a bit about spiritual development. I use it interchangeably with personal development and for me it means *a continuous practice of evolving as an individual in a way that supports the world in being a better place*. Individual development raises the collective consciousness of the world – the positive *vibe* or vibrational level of the universe. David R. Hawkins, M.C., Ph.D. goes into detail about this proven phenomenon in his ground-breaking book entitled *Power vs. Force*.

Spirituality isn't necessarily religious, although it can be as it is a unique practice for each of us. Personal or spiritual development is foundational for authentic leadership. Living in an integrated way in all parts of our life from the three centers of intelligence is a foundational practice as outlined in *The Wisdom of the Enneagram: The Complete Guide to Psychological and Spiritual Growth for the Nine Personalities* by Don Richard Riso, Russ Hudson.

Detailed Descriptions of the Three Centers of Intelligence

The Body center of intelligence

The body plays a crucial role in all forms of genuine spiritual work because bringing awareness back to the body anchors the quality of Presence. The reason is… while our minds and feelings can wander to the past or the future, our body can only exist here and now, in the present moment. This is one of the fundamental reasons why virtually all meaningful spiritual work begins with coming back to the body and becoming more grounded in it. The instincts of the body are the most powerful energies that we have to work with. Any real transformation must involve them…[17]

The Heart center of intelligence

At the deepest level, your heart qualities are the source of your identity. When your heart opens, you know who you are, and that *who you are* has nothing to do with what people think of you and nothing to do with your past history. You have a particular quality, a flavor, something that is unique and intimately you. It is through the heart that we recognize and appreciate our true nature.[18]

---

16 The Wisdom of the Enneagram – The Complete Guide to Psychological and Spiritual Growth for the Nine Personality Types", Don Richard Riso and Russ Hudson, c 1999, p 52.

17 Ibid, p 51.

18 Ibid, p 55.

INTEGRATING THE THREE CENTERS OF INTELLIGENCE

The Head center of intelligence:

The quiet mind is the source of inner guidance that gives us the ability to perceive reality exactly as it is. It allows us to be receptive to an inner knowing that can guide our actions. Just as we are seldom fully in our bodies or in our hearts, we seldom have access to the quiet, spacious quality of the mind. Quite the contrary, for most of us, the mind is an inner chatterbox, which is why people spend years in monasteries or in retreats trying to quiet their restless minds.[19]

Each of us lives from one of these centers of intelligence in particular and we are able learn to bring in the other two more of the time.[20] What is your preferred center of intelligence?

Integrating authenticity into our leadership improves awareness and makes us more effective

In the world where ambiguity and newness of experience are the norm, where creativity of new paradigms are made, and metaphors and languages are called for,[21] an integrated way of living is helpful. Margaret Wheatley, in her book, *Leadership and the New Science*, talks about the nature of the leadership work she and others are undertaking:

I was in this work a few years before I was able to identify its real nature. I realized that I and others weren't asking people simply to adopt some new approaches to leadership, or to think about organizations in a few new ways. What we were really asking, and what was also being asked of us, was that we change our thinking at the most fundamental level, that of our world view. The dominant world view of Western culture... doesn't help us to live well in this world any longer. We have to see the world differently if we are to live in it more harmoniously.[22]

In the book, *Slowing Down to the Speed of Life* by Richard Carlson and Joseph Bailey, the authors talk about two modes of thinking — frantic, analytical, computer-like and creative, free-flow. If you think of a child and how they can play for hours, or a time when you were doing something you love and before you knew it, it was several hours later — this is creative free-flow. It's called *being present* and requires less effort as we easily connect in the moment to our creativity and our authentic self.

As we move into adulthood, we become socialized to do what is valued, to focus on our productivity, to get more done with less, and to add technology into the mix so we can get even more done. Eventually, we become used to the frantic, busy, computer-like mode of thinking.

For effective leadership and to support our well-being, we need to remember or relearn the creative free-flow way of being and build our capacity to be choice-ful. When we step into the busy-ness, we can remember that we have the ability to step back and live in the second, or free-flow mode, more of the time.

The importance of this ability cannot be understated.

When we listen to and integrate our three centers of intelligence, in every moment, we are connected to our authentic self through the creative free-flow mode of thinking or being. We open to our inner purpose, we know who we are and what is truly important to us, and we live in the present moment as we cultivate the quality of *presence*.

As you learn to allow your personal integrity to be your guide, your sense of feeling alone will vanish.

---

19 Ibid, p 58.

20 Ibid, p 49 – 60. Note, the three centers of intelligence are also called the Instinctive Triad.

21 Leadership and the New Science, Margaret Wheatley, 1999

22 Ibid, p 172.

Your personal will can then emerge so that you will stand in your truth.[23]

Authentic leaders open to their emotional intelligence. This is a differentiator in the world for leaders, whether in business or outside of it. In the presence of authenticity others *are inspired to be truer to themselves.*[24]

People want to be around leaders who are able to be real, able to live as their authentic selves rather than through automatic patterns and habits of personality. Clients, employees, family and friends can sense this. Authentic leaders exude a sense of calm and confidence and live in the world from a place of integrity and wisdom.

We can learn to integrate each of these into our leadership and our lives

How do we actually do this? The path is similar and unique for each of us.

What is similar for everyone is that we each make a choice to grow as an individual and to enter into a life-long path of development. What is not the same is that the path is different for each one of us. Each of us has a different personality with unique qualities, strengths, automatic patterns and beliefs. We can learn to be who we truly are as we relax the patterns and beliefs of personality. This is the work of personal development. Or the joy of it — it all depends on how you see it.

We live each day as a practice in showing up, being present, listening to each of our three centers of intelligence for guidance and leading in each moment anchored to our authentic self or our essence, who we are when we are at our best.

Specifically, the path of development includes:

- Find your way of slowing your body and becoming aware of your mind in order to listen and sense what is true for you. For example, meditation or a simple sitting practice;
- Understand your personality type and preferred center of intelligence using whatever assessments are helpful, including the Enneagram, a nine-point model which is a twenty-five-hundred-year-old personality system that crosses genders and cultures. It works at both the external level of behaviors and the inner level of automatic patterns and beliefs. Reflect on and review your own life story and conduct interviews with friends and family to do the same;
- Get support where you feel the need — a coach, therapist, mentor — whoever can support you with the rough spots of your development journey, where you can't seem to find a way forward on your own;
- Be open to developmental opportunities each day and to each new learning edge that appears;
- Find practices for developing the capacity to open to and integrate each of the centers of intelligence (suggestions follow);
- Learn new ways of seeing the world in order to open up possibilities for thought;
- Continuously develop your self-awareness, as well as, new habits and beliefs;
- Celebrate your progress, and have compassion when things go differently than you expected; remember we're in this for the long-term. Development can continue until we cease to exist.

When we do this, we experience abundance, wellness, and inner peace more of the time

Other people can sense authenticity in leaders and the tangible benefits are many:

---

23 Jamie Sams and David Carson, Medicine Cards — The Discover of Power through the ways of Animals, 1999, p 134.

24 "The Authentics", Oprah Magazine, March 2007.

- Satisfied clients because leaders are able to keep their perspective in times of stress, as well as, increase creativity when original thought is required;
- Engaged employees because leaders are able to let down their defenses and be themselves which employees experience as approachability thus feel safe to speak their truth;
- Better decision making because leaders learn to create an environment that values diversity of thought;
- Increased effectiveness as leaders become aware of and move beyond old, automatic patterns, and beliefs that may be limiting their leadership.

We can sense the shifts in ourselves as we live in an integrated way and open to our full potential. Examples of the positive effects of long-term improved performance while maintaining personal wellness and alignment to our authentic self, include:

- More perspective during times of stress;
- Increased capacity to stay present in situations and with people where, in the past, we would get startled, confused or *thrown*;
- Improved energy as we relax old, automatic patterns;
- Improved creativity as we tap into our intuition more of the time;
- More inner peace as we live in alignment with our inner purpose;
- Less fear and more joy: Improved wellness; Improved results.

ACTION STEPS

Reflections

Each of us lives from one of these centers of intelligence in particular and we can learn to bring the other two in more of the time.

- What is your preferred center of intelligence?[25]

- You know this because of the following:

Practices

Use the following Self Observations and Practices to support you to integrate your three centers of intelligence

Simple Mindful Sitting

When you practice mindful sitting, you do a number of things:
- You develop the observer or ability to observe both yourself in any situation and what is going on internally in the moment. For example, you might observe that you are in a difficult conversation with a friend while internally feeling that you are becoming uncomfortable. You feel fear and assume the interaction will end well because you trust your friend deeply;
- You calm your nervous system;

---
[25] Ibid, p 49 – 60. Note, the three centers of intelligence are also called the Instinctive Triad.

- You support your personal wellness.

Instructions for a Mindful Sitting Practice: [26]
- Begin by sitting up straight in your chair and putting your feet flat on the ground. Place your hands on your knees and soften your gaze at a forty-five-degree angle to the floor. You can close your eyes if you like. Focus attention on your breath. Feel it go in and out; feel it at the entry point of your nose;
- When you notice thoughts come and go, label them as *thoughts* in your mind and gently bring your attention back to your breath. Notice noises around you that occur in the room, building, or outside and gently come back to your breath;
- Practice this daily between meetings in a room where you can lock the door and not be disturbed. Choose a time that supports you best — at the beginning of your day to ease into it or anytime and anywhere you need to rest and relax.

Notice and Name your feelings:

Check in once a week for the next three months for ten minutes and, using the following list of words that describe feelings, reflect on these questions in your journal:

- During the week, when did you notice you felt off in your interactions with others? Choose one particular situation for this practice;
- Refer to the list below and note what feeling(s) you experienced in the interaction;
- How do you know this was the feeling? What was the sensation associated with the feeling and where did you feel it in your body? For example, I felt stress as a tightening in my shoulders and a tenseness in my forehead;
- What did you learn about yourself as a result?

---

[26] Adapted from "A Path with Heart", Jack Kornfield.

List of feeling words:[27]

Pleasant feelings

open	passionate	cheerful	impulsive
understanding	admiration	sunny	free
confident	warm	merry	frisky
reliable	touched	elated	animated
easy	sympathy	jubilant	spirited
amazed	close	interested	thrilled
free	happy	concerned	wonderful
sympathetic	great	affected	positive
interested	gay	fascinated	eager
satisfied	joyous	intrigued	keen
receptive	lucky	absorbed	earnest
accepting	fortunate	inquisitive	intent
kind	delighted	nosy	anxious
love	overjoyed	snoopy	inspired
loving	gleeful	alive	determined
considerate	thankful	playful	excited
affectionate	important	courageous	enthusiastic
sensitive	festive	energetic	bold
tender	ecstatic	liberated	brave
devoted	satisfied	optimistic	daring
attracted	glad	provocative	challenged

27 http://www.psychpage.com/learning/library/assess/feelings.html

Difficult/Unpleasant feelings

angry	dull	repugnant	wronged
irritated	nonchalant	despicable	alienated
enraged	neutral	disgusting	confused
hostile	reserved	abominable	upset
insulting	weary	terrible	doubtful
sore	bored	in despair	uncertain
annoyed	preoccupied	sulky	indecisive
upset	cold	bad	perplexed
hateful	disinterested	a sense of loss	embarrassed
unpleasant	lifeless	afraid	hesitant
offensive	threatened	fearful	shy
bitter	cowardly	terrified	stupefied
aggressive	quaking	suspicious	disillusioned
resentful	depressed	anxious	unbelievable
inflamed	lousy	alarmed	skeptical
provoked	disappointed	panic	distrustful
incensed	discouraged	nervous	misgiving
infuriated	ashamed	scared	lost
cross	powerless	worried	unsure
worked up	diminished	frightened	uneasy
fuming	guilty	timid	pessimistic
indignant	dissatisfied	shaky	tense
indifferent	miserable	restless	hurt
insensitive	detestable	doubtful	crushed

tormented	dejected	afflicted	agonized
deprived	rejected	aching	appalled
pained	injured	victimized	humiliated
tortured	offended	heartbroken	

Journal weekly:

Journal about what you are learning as a result of these self-observation exercises. Ask yourself what information you are receiving as a result of your new awareness. Reflect on how this is supporting you in being more effective as a leader, with family and friends.

After three months, reflect on the following in your journal:

- Write down three times during the three months where you noticed you listened and integrated all three centers of intelligence into your day-to-day living. How do you know you integrated each of them?
- What have you learned about yourself? How has this supported you in your leadership? In your life? What can you do differently as a result?

Reflect in your journey for ten minutes about how all these practices can support you to be a more effective leader in business. And more effective as a person in all parts of your life.

Arc of Intense Energy Reflection

Refer to the diagram and description of the Arc of Intense Energy on page 17. Reflect on the topic of this chapter — integrating the three centers of intelligence. Answer the following questions in order to understand how the arc is showing up for you:

What is your old, automatic pattern when triggered? For example, *When I am triggered in a meeting with executives where I was asked a question I had no idea of the answer to, I freeze and get confused and respond ineffectively. I then go away and feel shame and lose my confidence.*

What is a new behaviour, belief or attitude you would like to choose instead? For example, *When I am triggered in a meeting with executives where I was asked a question I had no idea of the answer to, I move my attention into my body to feel my emotions and notice the sensations arising. I slow and deepen my breathing, write down my thoughts, and respond confidently saying may I get back to you on that.*

Practice self-managing through the arc when you are learning about this topic. Begin by paying attention; noticing the energy or discomfort intensifying in the body. As this occurs, practice relaxing your shoulders and belly and deepen and slow your breathing.

This will allow you to feel the emotions as they arise, notice your thoughts and discern if they are aligned with your values or just old, unhelpful messages.

When you learn to discern which is true and right, you will be able to maintain your perspective and choose a response that is appropriate, and authentic, for the situation at hand.

Remember your responses to these two questions. Practice using the new behaviour, belief or attitude as your response when triggered.

After a few weeks of practicing, reflect on what you are learning and how you will adjust your thoughts and behaviours as a result.

Closing reading

Most of us in modern societies are almost entirely estranged from the wisdom of our bodies. The psychological term for this is dissociation, in everyday language we call this checking out. In a busy, stress-filled day, it is likely we sense our body only if it is in pain. For instance, we do not usually notice we have feet unless our shoes are too tight. Even though our back is highly sensitive, we are usually unaware of it unless we are getting a massage or have a sunburn or a back injury — and sometimes not even[28]

---

[28] Riso and Hudson, "The Wisdom of the Enneagram", p 52.

Margaret Wheatley came to Vancouver for a luncheon after the launch of her book *Leadership and the New Science* and I was deeply impacted by her message that we needed to change our world view in order to create new ways to lead for the future.

I realized early on in my career that the world needed course corrections if we were to flourish as a species, and that each of us could play a part in this through our leadership within organizations, as well as, outside work in our families and communities.

This worksheet is an abbreviated version of the *Authentic You™ Personal Planning Process,* that I outlined in my first book *Awaken Your Authentic Leadership — Lead with Inner Purpose and Clarity*. And I still thought there was a place for it in the conversation series. Come to think of it, I may have written it before I published the book as a way to share my thinking before I did.

Discovering New Models for Leadership

— Action Worksheet —

> **Topic Description:**
>
> *I'm not comfortable with the old rules;*
> *they don't feel like a good fit for me anymore!*
>
> *How can I support organizational leadership being different in the 21st century?*
> *What needs to change?*

Use the following worksheet to develop your ability to lead from authentic self, more of the time, and to bring your way of being into your organization and your life.

Some of What the 21st Century is Bringing to Leaders Includes:

- A deadly global pandemic to add to the focus on climate change and the environment;
- An openness to spirituality and living aligned with our purpose in life;
- An increased number of women taking leadership roles in their communities;
- A labour market challenge where companies are beginning to look globally for employees;
- A focus on diversity as a business advantage;
- Technology supporting our lives and our businesses as well as speeding them up;
- A diversity in generations that is causing organizations to open to new ways of being (Millennials, Generation Y, X, Baby Boomers, etc.);
- Global financial system challenges.

It's a challenging time in the world and like generations past, a place of creativity and opportunity for new paradigms. Regarding leadership, each of us is being called upon to lead, no matter who we are or what we do.

I believe that we have only just begun the process of discovering and inventing the new organizational forms that will inhabit the 21st century. To be responsible inventors and discoverers, we need the courage to let go of the old world, to relinquish most of what we have cherished, to abandon our interpretations about what does and doesn't work. We must learn to see the world anew. As Einstein is often quoted as saying: No problem can be solved from the same consciousness that created it.[29]

In Order to Create the Way Forward for Leadership in the 21st Century:

- Make choices about your character by being clear about who you are and being open to your own guidance as you lead the way forward through uncharted waters;
- Make choices about your positive contribution by translating your values into your leadership principles and being clear about how you want to contribute in the world;

---

29 "Leadership and the New Science — Discovering Order in a Chaotic World, p 7, Margaret J. Wheatley.

- Create a strong foundation of support as you live the change you wish to see in the world;
- Create a daily practice to bring these alive in your life and your organization.

Make choices about your character and remember your authentic self:

Authenticity includes the following:

- The ability to be genuine and consistent in every part of your life;
- In each moment, have the ability to choose an appropriate response after taking in the information provided, allow and feel your emotions, listen to what your body is sensing, notice thoughts, judgments, and automatic patterns that may distort your interpretation, and discern what is real and what is old and unnecessary to consider;
- In each day, have the ability to manifest your leadership and your life in ways that are congruent and aligned with who you are as authentic self and with a global, ethical context.

ACTION STEPS

Reflections

Be clear about who you are as authentic self and listen to your inner wisdom, so you can lead yourself and others forward through uncharted waters. Use the spaces below to reflect on the following:

- Write down five–ten words that describe who you are when at your best or living congruent with your essence or authentic self. Use any assessments to understand your personality and what aspects are your strengths and support you in being at your best. For example, Enneagram, Myers Briggs, Insights, StrengthsFinder, etc.:

- Ask three people you know well in your life what your gift is or what you were *intended* for on this earth. Write it here:

- If you are not yet aware, it can be helpful to become aware of the aspects of personality that may be getting in the way of you stepping into your full power as a leader. For example, *My need for control and lack of genuine trust in my employees means that I find it difficult to delegate and therefore I micromanage and/or do it all myself.*

  Note: After shifting some of these and spending more time as authentic self, as well as, researching what makes you happy and feel alive while paying attention to when your energy builds and when it drains within certain activities, your gift or what you were intended for can become clearer.

  Activities where your energy builds:

  Activities where your energy drains:

  Aspects of personality that it may be helpful for you to shift:

- Research what you can do to understand what others are doing that is their gift or purpose and how it is for them to be living each day as they share this with others

Practices

Make choices about your positive contribution by translating your values into your leadership principles:

- Values are underlying general basic beliefs about what is good, desirable or worthwhile;
- They are abstract and general;
- They are believed to be what people care about deeply and serve as standards for judging acts, guiding behavior, evaluating social conditions, and give meaning to life;
- Values are thought to be relatively stable, much longer lasting and less subject to change than opinions so they are not subject to sudden shifts or impulses of the moment;
- Finally, it is thought that they can be ranked in order of importance."[30]

Transfer your values here from the *Leading from your Values* Action Worksheet.

Begin to articulate what your vision is for your life

Find clarity about your vision and how you can be of service to your organization and the world. If you don't know, it can be helpful to create a Vision Board as a starting point. To do this, use a poster board and several magazines as well as tape and scissors. Get comfortable, make sure you have about two hours available in a private space and put on your favorite music.

- Ask yourself, *What do I want more of in my life? How do I want it to feel each day? What activities do I want to be doing that are both good for the world, and that feed my soul?*
- Then look through the magazines and notice which images, words, colors call to you or that you are drawn to. Cut them out. When you are ready and have enough of them, place them on the poster board and tape them down. Let this tell the story of your life and how you choose to live it going forward;
- Share it with someone close and notice how it feels when you do. What is the emotion you are feeling? How does your Vision Board make you feel?
- Spend time with your Vision Board on a regular basis and allow the action steps to unfold. Take the next step, learn, reflect on your board, wait, and take the next step…

Make choices about your positive contribution

Translate all of these things, who you are, what your gift is, what you value and your vision for how you want to live your life into your leadership principles. In order to clarify your leadership principles, it can be helpful to reflect on how your values translate into action.

---

[30] Source: http://www.orednet.org/~jflory/205/205_val_intro.htm

For example, if you personally value sustainability, then this can translate into your leadership principles in a number of ways:

- You could support the creation of a team to green the office practices;
- You could provide ceramic cups and cutlery in the office kitchen;
- If you value authenticity, you could translate this into creating the space for meaningful dialogue with your team at work.

This will provide guidance for how you want to lead on a day-to-day basis.

Write your leadership principles here:

Make a simple plan for integrating these principles into to your leadership. This may take time and they may be integrated in a different order than you may think. Be open to the possibilities for new ways of being as a leader. Reflect and adjust as you go along.

Create a daily practice to bring these principles to your life and your organization:

- Support and work with others;
- Organize and operate your business or organization, your home or volunteer position with collaboration, co-creation, and partnerships;
- Create an environment where others can be who they are, speak their truth, and bring their creativity alive each day.
- Three things you can do differently now that you are clear about your leadership principles:

Create a strong personal foundation as you act as an agent of change in the world

- Write down the foundational practices that you either have in place, or will put in place to support you to lead authentically more of the time:

- Write down the people and communities of support you can participate in to have a safe place to be your authentic self and to get stronger so you can bring this into the world:
  People who you can be your authentic self around:

- Your communities of support:

Arc of Intense Energy Reflection

Refer to the diagram and description of the Arc of Intense Energy on page 17. Reflect on the topic of this chapter — discovering new models for leadership. Answer the following questions in order to understand how the arc is showing up for you:

What is your old, automatic pattern when triggered? For example, *When I am triggered by a leader who is instilling fear in her/his team in order to get things done, I get frustrated and angry though do not say or do anything.*

What is a new behaviour, belief or attitude you would like to choose instead? For example, *When I am triggered by a leader who is instilling fear in her/his team in order to get things done, I feel my frustration and anger, understand that it is because of my awareness of this injustice. I set up time to have a difficult conversation with the leader to provide feedback about my experience of her/him.*

Practice self-managing through the arc when you are learning about this topic. Begin by paying attention; noticing the energy or discomfort intensifying in the body. As this occurs, practice relaxing your shoulders and belly and deepen and slow your breathing.

This will allow you to feel the emotions as they arise, notice your thoughts and discern if they are aligned with your values or just old, unhelpful messages.

When you learn to discern which is true and right, you will be able to maintain your perspective and choose a response that is appropriate, and authentic, for the situation at hand.

Remember your responses to these two questions. Practice using the new behaviour, belief or attitude as your response when triggered.

After a few weeks of practicing, reflect on what you are learning and how you will adjust your thoughts and behaviours as a result.

Closing reading

The most important thing about leadership is your character and the values that guide your life. If you are guided by an internal compass that represents your character and the values that guide your decisions, you're going to be fine. Let your values guide your actions and don't ever lose your internal compass, because everything isn't black and white. There are a lot of grey areas in business and in life.[31]

---

31 Sara Lee CEO Brenda Barnes, in "True North — Discover your Authentic Leadership", p xxiv.

I remember the first time I had to fire an employee. I was hosting the first large-scale Business Trade Show in Revelstoke in my role as the Manager of the Chamber of Commerce. Having to let someone go was awful — gut wrenching. I was incredibly uncomfortable and yet I followed through with it because it was the right thing to do. Once I did, I noticed a metaphorical and actual sigh of relief by the rest of the team as they noticed this individual's bad behaviour and waited for me to lead the way to do something about it.

Development of this skill saved me as a leader as I experienced a range of performance-improvement conversations throughout my career. I believed that if I created the conditions, believed wholeheartedly that the employee could change, and they chose to behave differently, I would see progress and the result would be positive.

If they didn't, then I did all I could to support them and, in the end, if they chose not to change, they were clearly not a right fit. In some cases, they created a toxic environment and it was the right decision to part ways.

This was my truth as an authentic leader.

Taking Ken Blanchard's *Situational Leadership*© course was a turning point for me when I learned there were different stages of the learning curve for performance development and that different kinds of leadership were needed for each in order to be successful. I recommend researching and reviewing these stages as context for working through this worksheet.

Having a Difficult Performance Conversation

— Action Worksheet —

> **Topic Description:**
> *How can I say that?*
>
> *How do I have a difficult conversation at work or where I volunteer with an employee or contractor about her/his poor performance?*

The following worksheet will support you to prepare you to have a difficult conversation with an employee where there is a performance issue. This assumes that you believe the person has the potential for improvement.[32]

Things to Consider When Thinking About Having Difficult Conversations[33]

Difficult Conversations Are:

- *Gifts* you will be given over and over again in our lives and building capacity for them can help us manage stress and minimize suffering;
- Confidence-building opportunities;
- Less difficult over time with support and practice.

A gift you will be given over and over again

- This is one thing in this life you can count on because there will always be times when you are invited to engage in difficult conversations. You have a couple of choices — you can choose to avoid them which was a strategy I employed for a long time. When I found myself in a situation where I felt *thrown*, scared, intimidated or unprepared, I employed my preferred *defense mechanism* of the day in order to cope. I cried, got confused, forgot what I wanted to say, or my favorite, shut down and withdraw. I had no idea at the time that this was what I was doing. Or you can choose to engage and build your capacity and skill;
- You may not know *how* to have these kinds of conversations. Learning that there are actual skills I could develop that would support me was quite a revelation for me. Some of these included learning how to prepare, both what I wanted to say and how I would say it, as well as my physical presence. I learned how to sit and I remembered to breathe I learned what to do if I felt the conversation was at a standstill or if the person began to yell; how to debrief and

---

[32] If the employee is the wrong person for the position, a different kind of conversation will be required, and it would likely include a series of conversations such as the one that follows, supported by your HR team.

[33] The kinds of difficult conversations I'm speaking about are ones where violence is not an issue. I assume that these conversations are the ones that take place in our leadership on a day-to-day basis. Having a conversation where there is fear for your physical safety requires a different discussion that we will not be undertaking here.

celebrate what I learned; how to be curious about judgments and assumptions I made that got in the way of me connecting with the other person; how to let down my walls and speak my truth — just say what I knew to be true and inquire from a place of curiosity versus defense. I learned about how to be compassionate for myself as I felt I was in the kindergarten class of how to have a difficult conversation when I was actually a senior manager and a business owner;

- Over time, and with lots of support, *I changed how I see these situations — from something I needed to avoid at all costs to gifts I was given that provide the next opportunity for my development*. They will always be there, just like the person I can't get along with at the office. There will always be one in a different body and with a different name. And each is a gift to learn about myself, about compassion, and about how I can choose to show up, or not. My personal goal is to make the right choice, not necessarily the easy one.

Each provides a confidence-building opportunity

- There are different situations you experience — sometimes you have to respond in the moment, and sometimes you have the luxury of time to prepare;
- Each time I encounter a situation where I know it will be difficult for me to speak my truth, I remember how it felt the last time I entered into one and made it through and the little glint of self-confidence I experienced as a result. Even if I may have only said half of what I wanted to say, the fact that I was able to stay in the conversation despite my dry throat, sweaty palms, and desire to turn and run out of the room, was an accomplishment — a baby step. And each baby step adds up; the progress is cumulative;
- I remember thinking, *Maybe I can do this; just maybe I am getting stronger as a leader*. This was powerful for me. It gave me confidence that I could handle the next one and the next.

Less difficult with support and practice

- Practice includes learning to relax into deep belly breathing which is quite the contrary to what we learned as children. *Suck in your tummy* was a phrase I learned in ballet when I was five. It stuck with me until I was forty-three when I re-learned how to relax my belly, take deep breaths, and stay present in the moment. This has been a savior to me in my journey to build capacity to have difficult conversations as it allows me to step back for a moment, re-center and be choice-ful in how I respond, and get clear about what I want say next;
- Practice also means *building new muscles* such as jotting down a few notes about your thoughts in the moment and declaring that you need a minute to regroup before proceeding. It can be helpful to take a break or step out of a conversation any time you feel uncomfortable in order to reestablish a safe space before proceeding. There are several ways to practice including preparing your thoughts, role playing with someone (person A) who will support you, then proceeding with the conversation (with person B), and debriefing with the supportive person (person A) once the conversation is complete.

Providing feedback is essential to the continued growth of your team members. By taking the time to have these conversations, you support them as well as yourself. By providing feedback on an ongoing basis, you enable them to progress, and there are no surprises on either side if the person is not a right fit.

ACTION STEPS

Several things you can do in preparation for the conversation, to support yourself during the conversation, and to reflect on learnings once you finish.

Prior to the Conversation

For the employee

Let her know that you will set up time to have a conversation about her performance. Ideally, these are scheduled once a quarter or at least two times per year with on-going feedback as needed. The objective is to support the employee in their development and to ensure that all issues are talked about and cleared as they arise. This way, at the end of the year when final discussions take place, both sides are aware of how the employee is doing.

Ideally, the employee has a job description, a performance plan for the year complete with business and personal goals. You ask them to prepare their results and thoughts on their performance and provide you with them prior to the meeting.

This worksheet can be used for both formal and informal performance feedback meetings. It is important to balance the feedback as the employee may have a strong inner critic — five to one is the ratio of positive to negative feedback that will feel balanced to an employee.

In addition, there is a specific Action Worksheet on receiving and giving feedback effectively which will support you to have these conversations as well.

Reflections

Reflect on the following questions as part of your preparation:
- Do you know how you come across to people in difficult conversations? Do you know what your automatic patterns are? How might these need to shift in order for you to create the conditions for this employee to feel safe and *hear* the message?

- Is the employee new to a position requiring additional direction? Or is he/she a high-achiever needing more information to do the job? Is she/he experiencing learning curves and in a natural stage where she/he is frustrated? Do you need to be directive or supportive or both?

Write down answers to the following and use them in the conversation with the employee:

- What is your intention for the relationship? Is it to terminate the position or to build a long-term trust-based relationship? What is your objective for the conversation? Is it to be supportive, directive, or to re-engage the employee?

- How do you want to set the context in the conversation to ensure they know you believe in them, that you are seeking positives, as well as, areas of opportunity?

- What are your expectations for the job? Have you communicated these or do you need to include them in this conversation? If not, write them here.

HAVING A DIFFICULT PERFORMANCE CONVERSATION

- In what areas is the employee doing well within the context of the job and your expectations?

- Where is the employee not meeting these expectations? Choose one to two key issues as too many can be overwhelming. Use specific examples of behaviors you observed or experienced to ground your assessment. Stick to the facts as they cannot be disputed. For example, *on Tuesday, November 4th, you arrived at 9:40 am and your shift began at 9:00 am.*
  Examples:

  Examples:

- How do you prefer the employee deals with these situations? Describe to them what success looks like. Be specific and clear. Give concrete examples.
- How does the employee feel about the conversation and about the feedback? Once you have provided it to him, check in as to ask how he is feeling;
- Ask him what challenges he might face in making these changes and what support he requires from you as his supervisor;
- Tell him what the next steps are and when you will check in with each other again. For example, will there be follow up in a month to check progress or will the next check in be at the regular quarterly meeting?
- Check his understanding by asking him what he is taking away from the conversation. He may

need to write notes and/or send you a confirmation email. By asking if he agrees or not, you will get a sense of whether or not you are on the same page. This is particularly important where there are communication issues because of a language barrier;
- Hold the employee accountable to the new behaviors right from when they are communicated. Recognize when they demonstrate the new behaviours in order to reinforce their progress.

Practices

Role play; practice prior to having the conversation

- Find a person who you trust and who can provide you with support and feedback for the conversation, someone who has the courage to tell you how you come across and will provide the feedback in a respectful way;
- Role play the situation and reflect on learnings;
- Adjust your approach as required.

Your foundational practices the day of the conversation

If you have foundational practices, these days are when they are most important to keep in place. They support you in having more capacity for these kinds of conversations:

- Get enough sleep;
- Ensure your nutrition supports you by eating what builds your energy, not what drains it or creates brain fog. This included drinking lots of water;
- Exercise and meditation can help calm the nervous system;
- Include any other practices you have in place like journaling, etc.

Practices to support you in being present to the conversation

If you find yourself getting nervous and your mouth gets dry, practice deep belly breathing. *It sounds out there, but it works!* Often when you are stressed, you tighten your stomach, your breathing becomes shallow, and you hunch up your shoulders. By relaxing and breathing you support yourself to stay clear when you are stressed. Keep breathing as you continue the conversation.

As you practice having these kinds of difficult conversations, your confidence and self-esteem builds. They do become less difficult over time.

Debrief and reflect on learnings

Either with the appropriate, confidential, person who supported you in the role play, or on your own, reflect on the situation and answer the following questions:

- What are one to three things you learned about yourself and this situation?

- One thing you did well:

- One thing you could do differently next time as a result of what you learned:

By seeing these experiences as opportunities to learn, you can more readily accept them as they come up and grow in your leadership, as well as, support your employees, just as you do.

Arc of Intense Energy Reflection

Refer to the diagram and description of the Arc of Intense Energy on page 17. Reflect on the topic of this chapter — having a difficult performance conversation. Answer the following questions in order to understand how the arc is showing up for you:

What is your old, automatic pattern when triggered? For example, *When I am triggered by an employee who is unkind and manipulating a team member in order to get things done, I get frustrated and angry though do not say or do anything.*

What is a new behaviour, belief or attitude you would like to choose instead? For example, *When I am triggered by an employee who is unkind and manipulating a team member in order to get things done, I notice my feelings of frustration and anger, get support from my manager or human resources colleague, and set up time to have a clear and firm, performance management conversation.*

Practice self-managing through the arc when you are learning about this topic. Begin by paying attention; noticing the energy or discomfort intensifying in the body. As this occurs, practice relaxing your shoulders and belly and deepen and slow your breathing.

This will allow you to feel the emotions as they arise, notice your thoughts and discern if they are aligned with your values or just old, unhelpful messages.

When you learn to discern which is true and right, you will be able to maintain your perspective and choose a response that is appropriate, and authentic, for the situation at hand.

Remember your responses to these two questions. Practice using the new behaviour, belief or attitude as your response when triggered.

After a few weeks of practicing, reflect on what you are learning and how you will adjust your thoughts and behaviours as a result.

Closing Reading

I feel so sentenced by your words,
I feel so judged and sent away,
Before I go, I've got to know
Is that what you mean to say?

Before I rise to my defense,
Before I speak in hurt or fear,
Before I build that wall of words,
Tell me, did I really hear?

Words are windows or they're walls,
They sentence us, or set us free.

There are things I need to say,
Things that mean so much to me,
If my words don't make me clear,
Will you help me to be free?

If I seemed to put you down,
If you felt I didn't care,
Try to listen through my words,
To the feelings that we share.[34]

---

[34] Adapted from Ruth Bebermeyer as quoted by Marshall B. Rosenberg, Ph.D. in "Nonviolent communication — A language of life", p1.

Learning about the law of attraction had a great impact on my life and my leadership. The fact that my mind was defaulting to the negative and that I had a choice in every moment was quite empowering and very helpful.

Awareness and the ability to manifest are foundational and are results of a practice of authenticity.

Once you become aware of something, it's interesting how you can't go back to being unaware. It's been illuminated and you notice it everywhere.

This happens with abundance. Once you know it's a possibility, it shows up more and more.

It was enlightening to remember I had a choice in every moment about my mindset and that the natural default was scarcity and negativity.

You also have this choice as an authentic leader.

Shifting Scarcity to Abundance Mindset

— Action Worksheet —

> **Topic Description:**
> *When will I ever feel I have enough?*
> *How does a scarcity versus abundance mindset impact my leadership and my life?*

The importance of abundance has been a learning for me on my journey to authentic leadership. I'm not sure if I needed to complete my work on a number of different issues before I could make space for this one, or if it was just it's time to emerge.

I've always been aware of people who are eternal optimists and those who seemed to find the negative within all situations. However, I never really paid attention to how both orientations were showing up in my own life. The following worksheet will assist you in becoming more aware of abundance as it relates to your leadership and your life. It will also support you in taking the first steps to beginning to lead, and live with a bit more abundance.

Things to Consider When Thinking About Abundance:
- At each moment, we can choose our orientation — the cup half full or cup half empty;
- The understanding that the laws of attraction can support abundance;
- We can learn to have the courage to allow abundance in all parts of our lives.

At each moment, we can choose our orientation — cup half full or cup half empty

I remember the first time I was told I needed to watch the movie, *What the Bleep do we know?*[35] I found it hard to understand and I wasn't really interested in it. Then a few months later I picked it up and tried again. The main point I got from it was that I could choose what my perspective was for situations that arose in each moment. I could be negative or I could rise above it and choose a positive perspective. I learned that my body and my responses were *hard wired* to patterns that I was reliving over and over in my life. Patterns I had no idea were going on. It is always amazing to me how once a new one is revealed, I can see it so clearly and I can't go back to being unconscious of it — no matter how much I would like to at times.

I didn't realize how much time I was spending in a negative mode until then — it was quite frightening. Or how I allowed it to keep me on the straight and narrow of *not* stepping into my power and how I used it as an excuse to allow me to play small in my life. I was an executive of a three-billion-dollar company with forty-five hundred employees and I belittled myself at every turn. I self-sabotaged from stepping into my true leadership until I became aware my orientation was towards scarcity and a negative perspective a lot of the time.

---
35 http://www.whatthebleep.com/whatthebleep/

What the Bleep taught me I could re-wire my orientation, right down to my chemical composition if I began to make different choices.

So, I began to be more intentional within more moments of each day — to choose health over sickness, abundance over scarcity, positive over negative. I remember a period in my life when I believe I was a hypochondriac as I was at the doctor almost every month in a year for this ailment or that. I chose to pay attention to all the things that could be wrong with me instead of making health a priority and making choices each day to support this alternative perspective bringing more of it into my life.

I began paying attention to my energy levels when I chose the positive and it was amazing how much lighter and more relaxed I felt when I did. I began being intentional about my choices and it had a huge impact when I chose the positive. For a whole year, I didn't need to go to the doctor — I realized I was actively cultivating health.

While there are many times when I notice the negative, what is different now is I can see it sooner, reframe my thoughts, let go of old patterns in the moment, and move on quickly. I realize now that I have been building my *muscle* for abundance.

The understanding of the laws of attraction can support abundance

A few years ago, I rented the movie *The Secret*[36] and was introduced to the laws of attraction. The message I took away from it was there is this law, like gravity, that operates around me all the time and I had no idea until that moment that it could have such an impact on my life. I attended a wonderfully simple and pragmatic session with Michael Losier, author of *Laws of Attraction*[37], and through conversations with others who are also of this mindset, I began to actively practice the choice towards an orientation to the positive in my leadership and my life.

The law of attraction is a matcher, simple and clear — if you think, believe, focus on, and talk about things that are positive, they will occur. And alternatively, if you pay attention to things that are going wrong in your life, the spiral may continue. From negative to positive, this is my choice more and more of the time.

Also, as you pay attention to proof, watch your positive use of language and reframe your thoughts, you will begin to *mind your vibe* as Michael Losier suggests.[38] It's amazing how abundance shows up.

I remember a very successful friend who owns a consulting firm saying, *There is so much work out there*, and she stood out for me from all the others I know who were competing for work. Her positive orientation carries over into how she runs her business and how she lives her life. When you realize there is enough of everything out there for all, attachment to competition releases its hold on you and collaboration takes its place.

I also remember the first time I realized that fear can't exist in my mind at the same time as when I become present to compassion, joy, and doing the right thing. I was meditating before my coaching certification process and was astounded when I stayed present for a fleeting two to three seconds at a time and my fears disappeared momentarily. During the certification process, we had to meet a new client, get to know her, design a program and coach her in front of eleven students and a panel of teachers, all in one and a half hours.

---

36 http://www.thesecret.tv/

37 The Laws of Attraction", Michael Losier, 2006.

38 Ibid.

I had a choice — I could either allow my anxiety to take over and self-sabotage or I could stay present to what was needed for the client in the moment and do the right thing. When I became aware, and made a choice for the latter, this veil seemed to drop around the two of us and my awareness of the others in the room melted away. What was right for her was the most important thing to me, and as I stayed present, joy and compassion became present for me. Fear loosened its hold and it was a huge realization for me that day.

Being present to abundance in the many forms it takes is essential to allowing it to show up in our lives.

We can learn to have the courage to allow abundance in all parts of our lives

I read the book, *The Courage to be Rich*[39] by Suze Orman, and the learnings for me continue. I learned that abundance takes many forms in our lives and its definition is relative to each of us. It's about so much more than money — family, friends, health, joy, etc. Its definition may also shift as we become clear about what is truly important and how much is enough.

At the time, I was a year into building my leadership business and wallowed in the *it's never going to happen* perspective. I worried about the lack of money rolling in and I allowed it to override trusting and doing the right thing. I needed to let go of my attachment to how much money I was going to make and learn to practice an abundance mindset.

I learned from Suze Orman's book that each of us has baggage around money that we need to be aware of and work through. I realized It's important to have a healthy respect for it. I needed to adapt a mindset of abundance rather than a need for an unrealistic dollar amount in my bank account that would never be enough.

I began a practice of gratitude and appreciation when I felt myself feeling fear around not having enough. I began paying attention to how much I have in my life, my health, my relationships with my family and friends, and all I am sincerely grateful for. Each time I shifted my orientation, I relaxed and felt lighter. Each time I would notice the next experience of abundance that was showing itself in my life.

I also had to learn to accept gifts people were offering me every day. *I'll pay for that* or *Let me do that for you* or *I love that skirt* were things I deflected and very, very rarely let the associated feelings of joy sink in. My belief was that I had to do it myself and I had to deflect a compliment given to me so I wouldn't appear arrogant. I took away a gift they wanted to give to me and I blocked abundance from showing up in these and other ways as a result.

My coach at the time asked me, *What would it be like for you if you had enough in your life right now? What would it be like if you lived your life from this perspective more of the time?* She provided a huge light beam shining directly on my old belief! I experienced an immediate relief and lightness that flooded my awareness and my body.

 I am still negative at times and move into my downward spirals, but what is different for me is I can become aware of it in the moment or soon afterwards and I can reframe my perspective making a choice for the positive allowing abundance to show itself once more.

A foundation of abundance has been essential as I learn to live with ease. It is a life-long journey and I am in the midst of it and have inner peace more than I ever experienced before. My definition of how much is enough has greatly shifted.

---

39 Suze Orman, "The Courage to be Rich: Creating a life of material and spiritual abundance", 1999.

ACTION STEPS

Reflections

The first step towards the mindset of abundance is to become aware of your relationship with abundance versus scarcity. Answer the following questions:

- While developing awareness about your current belief surrounding abundance, what is your personal opinion about the difference regarding scarcity versus abundance?

- What is your dominant perspective in life and in your leadership? Scarcity (there will never be enough) or Abundance (there is always enough)? How do you know?

- How is scarcity showing up for you in your leadership? For example, *I am afraid to make decisions on new projects as we'll never have enough money, and if we have the money, we won't have the people.* Or, *I'm unhappy with my life and that has an impact on each person I meet throughout the day.* Also, how is it showing up in other aspects of your life?

- How is abundance showing up in your leadership?

- How is it showing up in other aspects of your life?

- If shifted, what beliefs or automatic patterns would support having just a little more abundance?

- What are you learning about yourself?

- What one thing can you do differently in order to have just a little more abundance in your life?

Practices

Incorporating a daily practice of gratitude and appreciation into your life

What can be helpful to shift your orientation to one of abundance is to incorporate a daily practice of gratitude and appreciation. This can be as simple as finding one thing about your life you are grateful for. Your natural orientation may be towards paying attention to the negative aspects of your experiences, so it may take time to build your muscle to rebalance these thoughts.

- Make a list of things you appreciate about yourself. For example, *I am grateful for my good health and that I'm able to help my friends when they need me*:

- Make a list of things, people, experiences, relationships …. you are grateful for in your life. For example, *I am grateful for my family, friends, my comfortable home, having enough food to eat, my job and the people I work for*:

- Read these statements over and notice how it feels to be grateful. What does it feel like? How do you know?

Taking action to live with more abundance each day

When you begin learning to choose abundance over scarcity, positive over negative, you learn to create a different way of thinking about your life; imagine re-hardwiring your brain to a new way that may feel uncomfortable if your automatic pattern, like many others, is to adopt a negative perspective most the time. Give yourself a chance. Remember it will take time and compassion as you begin these practices.

- Watch your language — using and instead of but where the word but in a sentence negates the first part of it. For example, *I like your project plan, and I'd make the following changes* rather than, *I like your project plan, but I'd change this, this and this.* Both aspects of the thought can exist at the same time.
    - Practice by writing a statement with *but* in it:

    - Now, write the same statement with *and* in it:

    - How does it feel different when you read each?

    - How would a person react when you change your language to include *and*?

- Begin to notice how many times a day you use *no, not, never or don't*.[40] The law of attraction says the universe doesn't hear these words so it will simply give you more of what you talk about when you say you don't want them. Practice reframing your statements to include what you do want more of in your life. For example, *I want to work with people who inspire me to be a better leader*, rather than, *There is no way I'm going to work with people who are intimidating and aggressive*.
  - Practice writing out a statement about something you don't want in your leadership. For example, *I'm not organized and I'm never able to manage all of my commitments*:

  - Now, reframe it to write a new statement about what you do want more of in your life. For example, *I'm in the process of learning how to manage my schedule more effectively given all the requests for back-to-back meetings*:

- Complete the following practice when you have something specific you want to manifest.[41] It can be something you want to occur today or at some point in the future:

  Step one: Use a blank piece of paper and in the center draw a circle. Inside the circle write down what you want to happen in the situation. For example, *the presentation I am making to our stakeholders is meaningful to them and strengthens our relationship*;

  Steps two to twelve: Draw a circle around the first circle and in it write down one thing that needs to occur in order for this to be true. For example, *I understand what is important to the stakeholders*; draw another circle around the last one and in this circle write down another thing that needs to occur in order for this to be true. For example, *I need to prepare my thoughts and practice prior to the presentation*.

---

40 Adaped from "The Law of Attraction – The Science of Attracting more of what you want and less of what you don't want", Michael Losier.

41 This may be a practice from the works of Esther Hicks on the laws of attraction. I learned about it at an authentic leadership session in Nanaimo, B.C. and am not sure of the exact source.

Other things that you might put in the circles:
- I get enough sleep the night before the presentation;
- I complete my foundational practices the day before and on the day of the presentation;
- I clarify my intention for the presentation with myself before I begin;
- I notice my assumptions during the presentation and either check them out, or rebalance them in the moment and let them go.

At the end you will have drawn twelve circles around your initial statement indicating what you want to occur. I'm not sure of the significance of the number of circles, just that when I do it, it seems to be enough to shift my negative beliefs about the situation so that I can actually begin to believe it will occur.

Notice how it feels to believe that what you want to occur, actually occurred. How does it feel in your body? For example, *It feels lighter and I feel warm*. What does it look like when it happens — imagine it in your mind, *I can see people coming up and telling me how it has positively impacted them and that makes me feel happy*.

Then, put this away and go on with your day. Take this renewed, positive *vibe* or energy into your day. Take actions that actually support this occurring in your life.

If what you want to occur is in the future, spend time with this sheet each morning in order to re-orient to the positive and to feel what it is like for it to already have occurred. This is a key step in practicing the law of attraction.

Use the rest of this page and the instructions outlined above to practice manifesting what you would like to occur:

Final Reflection

While practicing choosing abundance, it can be helpful to keep a journal and pay attention to proof, or evidence for your mind, of when it occurs in your life:

- For the next three months, begin to pay attention to and document proof of abundance in your life;
- In your journal, create a section for recognizing when and how abundance shows up. Share your reflections with a friend or with your significant other;
- Notice how you feel as you reflect on abundance.

Arc of Intense Energy Reflection

Refer to the diagram and description of the Arc of Intense Energy on page 17. Reflect on the topic of this chapter — shifting scarcity to abundance mindset. Answer the following questions in order to understand how the arc is showing up for you:

What is your old, automatic pattern when triggered? For example, *When I am triggered by a change in the organizational structure where another department gets more resources for a high-priority project, I become afraid there won't be enough to support my team and notice anger and jealousy towards the manager of the other team.*

What is a new behaviour, belief or attitude you would like to choose instead? For example, *When I am triggered by a change in the organizational structure where another department gets more resources for a high-priority project, I notice my anxiety about there not being enough, and my jealousy. I let it go, knowing it's just my inner critical voice, and I congratulate the manager of the other team.*

Practice self-managing through the arc when you are learning about this topic. Begin by paying attention; noticing the energy or discomfort intensifying in the body. As this occurs, practice relaxing your shoulders and belly and deepen and slow your breathing.

This will allow you to feel the emotions as they arise, notice your thoughts and discern if they are aligned with your values or just old, unhelpful messages.

When you learn to discern which is true and right, you will be able to maintain your perspective and choose a response that is appropriate, and authentic, for the situation at hand.

Remember your responses to these two questions. Practice using the new behaviour, belief or attitude as your response when triggered.

After a few weeks of practicing, reflect on what you are learning and how you will adjust your thoughts and behaviours as a result.

Closing Reading

You tell the world who you are a thousand times a day. But that's not all.

The world receives your gifts, whatever they may be, and sends them right back to you.

Your thoughts become words. Your words become actions.

And, your actions have an effect from one person to another…

In a sense each of us creates the world over and over again, a thousand times a day.

In this respect, you can live a rich life or a poor one and it won't make one bit of difference whether you have a lot of money or none at all.[42]

---

42 From "The Courage to be Rich"(2002), pg 404 by Suze Orman

Living congruent with your values is foundational for authenticity. In order to live true to your deepest beliefs, it is helpful to become conscious of them, to write them down, and to consider them when making decisions.

Sometimes, your values will align completely with the organization you work within and with others, there will be a misalignment. This is the time to ask the big questions which include, *Who am I and what do I truly want in my life and leadership*. If the organization espouses certain values and doesn't actually adhere to them, it causes tension to arise and it may be time to either support change from within or to make a choice to leave.

In any event, values provide a starting point for being true to yourself in your leadership and your life.

This is the second worksheet that is similar to the one in my first two books. Again, it is helpful to complete as part of this book, in case you do not have the others.

Leading and Living Congruent With Your Values

— Action Worksheet —

> **Topic Description:**
>
> *That's a tricky one!*
> *How do I live congruent with my values, especially in difficult situations?*

The following worksheet will assist you to become more aware of your values as they relate to your leadership and your life. It will also support you in taking the first steps to begin to lead and live congruent with what is deeply important to you.

Things to Consider Regarding Bringing Your Values into Your Day-To-Day Decision-Making:

- Know what your values are;
- Bring them out when you are making decisions;
- Get support if you aren't sure;
- Learn from the situation so you can adjust your approach the next time.

Know what your values are

Values are deeply held beliefs about what is important to you and how you want to live. Essentially, they are your *bottom line*. Spend some time articulating them and keep them with you. Share your values and have a conversation about them with others. This helps to deepen your understanding and commitment to them. Check them against other possible values to understand tradeoffs and ensure these are the most important ones for you.

Bring them out when you are making decisions

There may be times where you encounter situations that require choice and action that isn't always easy. And there will be times of opportunity that require difficult choice as well. Some include:

- Seeing a co-worker behave in a way that is unethical;
- Being approached by a supervisor in a way you are not comfortable with;
- Being put in a situation that creates a conflict of interest;
- Behaving in a way that isn't congruent with your values when under stress or having a bad day. You may make a mistake and not realize it until after you did it;
- You may be faced with an incredible opportunity and need to make a decision that could change your life.

Your values will help you navigate these.

When you have a decision to make and aren't sure of the way to approach it, you can bring out your values and think about the situation in the context of them. Each value can provide a guidepost and together they can provide a north start to navigate by.

For example, if you are presented with a new business or job opportunity and aren't sure if it is right for you, you could check it against your values — use them as criteria to evaluate the opportunity. If it is a position requiring eighty hours a week including weekly travel around the world and you have a value of adventure, it might be the right position for you. If you have a value of the importance of spending time with family, locally and on a regular basis, it might not be a good fit for you.

I'll never forgot the first time the CEO I was working for brought out the company values in an executive meeting and had us walk through a very controversial decision in the context of each. It was clear where we had done the right thing and also clear where we could have done things a bit differently. It caused each of us to sit back and reflect about how to go forward.

Get support when you're not sure

If you work for a company with a code of conduct advisor, call them. Ask your boss or human resources representative for confidential advice. If you are an entrepreneur, call a friend who's a lawyer or someone who has been a role model for high ethical standards and ask them for support. Call the labour relations board or other advisory body. They can provide thoughtful insights and an objective perspective for what could be a stressful, complex situation. You can take the guidance that feels right and still make the final decision yourself.

Learn from the situation so you can adjust your approach the next time

Each time I approach a situation where I'm unclear about how to navigate, I do the best I can with the information and resources I have at the time. I'm more ok at this point in my life that I may not always get it right. I'm much more compassionate with myself when I don't. I do, however, try to fix the situation and make amends with those involved when I act in a way that is not congruent with my values.

When I'm out of alignment I know it right away. My body tells me there's something that's not right. I get a sick feeling in my stomach and a grey mood comes over me as I go over and over the situation in my mind. I don't sleep if there is a conversation I need to have. I notice my discomfort in knowing I will have to fess up and make amends. I also notice I am proud of myself when I do.

Knowing there will always be more opportunities to practice, I reflect and learn from the situation so I can change my approach the next time. And then I let it go.

ACTION STEPS

Reflections

Use the following exercise to develop an awareness of your values:

Become aware of what values are — the underlying general basic beliefs about what is good, desirable or worthwhile:

- Values are abstract and general;
- They are believed to be what people deeply care about and serve as standards for judging acts, guiding behavior, evaluating social conditions, and give meaning to life;
- Values are thought to be relatively stable, much longer lasting and less subject to change than opinions so they are not subject to sudden shifts or impulses of the moment;
- Finally, it is thought that they can be ranked in order of importance.

Source: http://www.orednet.org/~jflory/205/205_val_intro.htm

Refer to the list of values words at the end of this Action Worksheet and make a list of your top six values:

- Reflecting on your values, what are you learning about yourself?

- What one thing can you do differently as a result?

Practices

Practice taking action to live in ways that are congruent with your values

- When you begin working with your values, you are learning to create a different way of thinking about your life. Imagine re-hardwiring your brain with a new way that may feel uncomfortable if your automatic pattern, like many others, is to live in ways that are not congruent with your values some of the time. Give yourself a chance. Remember it will take time and having compassion for yourself will support you as you begin these practices.
    - Write down a current situation where you are living in a way that is congruent with your values:

    - How do you know? What is the feeling or emotion you feel when you live aligned with who you are and what is important to you? For example, *I feel joy and at peace*:

    - Write down a current situation where you are living in a way that is not congruent with your values:

LEADING AND LIVING CONGRUENT WITH YOUR VALUES

- Again, how do you know? What does it feel like when you are out of alignment with your values? For example, *I feel depressed and there is a hollow feeling in my chest*:

- What can you do differently in your life to live more fully aligned with your values?

- Understanding and living in line with your values provides you with internal guidance and intrinsic motivation. It supports you to live or lead during times when you are unsure of the next step going forward. You can bring your values out and consider the situation within the context of them. For example, if you value integrity and family, as well as, a strong work ethic, then there may be tradeoffs you need to make if your boss wants you to work evenings and weekends. Being clear about your values will provide guideposts for your boundaries and for conversations you may need to have in order to live congruent with them. It also supports you to be clear during times of conflict or when group think may be taking place, as well as, when you need to set a boundary because someone else's behaviour is not aligned with your values. Reflect on the following questions and identify simple actions you can take to live aligned with your values:
    - What can you do at work to bring your values into your leadership? For example, *I value authenticity so I can begin to have real conversations with my team and speak my truth, particularly when they may disagree*.

- How would it support your team if they understood your values?

- How would it support your team members if you understood their values?

- How would it support your family members, or friends, if you understood their values?

- How would it support you if they understood yours?

LEADING AND LIVING CONGRUENT WITH YOUR VALUES

Using your values to set a boundary

Boundaries are a way of defining what is acceptable to you and what is not.

It can be helpful to be clear about a new boundary when you get the sense that a situation or person's behaviour is out of alignment with your values. You may get an uncomfortable feeling before you are able to clearly articulate what it is that is not working for you. Use the following exercise to gain clarity, and to help you prepare for a difficult conversation you may need to have.

Think of a particular situation at work — let's say how you want to spend a typical work week. Draw a circle[43] and write all that is acceptable to you inside the circle and all that is not, or that is acceptable if you invite it in, outside the circle. Once done, you will see the line of your boundary and you'll be clearer about what you want to accept and what you may not.

Inside the Circle

1. **What is acceptable to me in this situation:**

    i.e. respectfully working together with people who inspire me to be better

2. **What is acceptable to me, if I invite it in:**

    i.e. working with a person I have a difficult time interacting with, where I get support to address it and they are willing to work on the relationship

Outside the Circle

What's not acceptable to me in this situation:

i.e. working with a bully and allowing it to affect my confidence and ability to do my job (not trying to address it)

---

43 Source: The Medicine Cards — learning about spirituality through animals — p 149

Use the following space to draw a circle and clarify your boundary:

Self-managing as a support for living congruent with your values when others may disagree

When you catch yourself unsure of a situation or person's behaviour and something feels weird or uncomfortable, you can practice self-managing to set a boundary in the moment or have a conversation to clarify what is not working for you. In order to self-manage, it can be helpful to understand how the Arc of Intense Energy works.

Arc of Intense Energy Reflection

Refer to the diagram and description of the Arc of Intense Energy on page 17. Reflect on the topic of this chapter — leading and living congruent with your values. Answer the following questions in order to understand how the arc is showing up for you:

What is your old, automatic pattern when triggered? For example, *When I am triggered by a contractor who I experience billing fees in a way that is inappropriate and against company policy, I notice anger rising and do nothing about it until the next time I see it happen.*

What is a new behaviour, belief or attitude you would like to choose instead? For example, *When I am triggered by a contractor who I experience billing fees in a way that is inappropriate and against company policy, I notice anger rising, remember my value of integrity and do the following — have confidence in the truth of my experience, tell my manager and set up a call with the Code of Conduct advisor to get coaching for how to approach the situation.*

Practice self-managing through the arc when you are learning about this topic. Begin by paying attention; noticing the energy or discomfort intensifying in the body. As this occurs, practice relaxing your shoulders and belly and deepen and slow your breathing.

This will allow you to feel the emotions as they arise, notice your thoughts and discern if they are aligned with your values or just old, unhelpful messages.

When you learn to discern which is true and right, you will be able to maintain your perspective and choose a response that is appropriate, and authentic, for the situation at hand.

Remember your responses to these two questions. Practice using the new behaviour, belief or attitude as your response when triggered.

After a few weeks of practicing, reflect on what you are learning and how you will adjust your thoughts and behaviours as a result.

Resources

Ethics and values in business:

The Ethical Mind, Harvard Business Review, March 2007.

Avoiding Integrity Landmines, Harvard Business Review, April 2007.

Closing Reading

You must be the change you wish to see in the world.

~ Gandhi

Values Words — Common Personal Values:

Accomplishment, Success	Discovery	Love, Romance	Satisfying others
Accountability	Ease of Use	Loyalty	Security
Accuracy	Efficiency	Maximum utilization (of time, resources)	Self-givingness
Adventure	Equality	Meaning	Self-reliance
All for one & one for all	Excellence	Merit	Simplicity
Beauty	Fairness	Money	Skill
Calm, quietude, peace	Faith	Openness	Speed
Challenge	Family	Peace, Non-violence	Spirit in life (using)
Change	Family feeling	Perfection (e.g. of details)	Stability
Cleanliness, orderliness	Flair	Personal Growth	Standardization
Collaboration	Freedom	Pleasure	Status
Commitment	Friendship	Positive attitude	Strength
Communication	Fun	Power	Succeed; A will to-
Community	Global view	Practicality	Success, Achievement
Competence	Good will	Preservation	Systemization
Competition	Goodness	Privacy	Teamwork
Concern for others	Gratitude	Problem Solving	Timeliness
Content over form	Hard work	Progress	Tolerance
Continuous improvement	Harmony	Prosperity, Wealth	Tradition

LEADING AND LIVING CONGRUENT WITH YOUR VALUES

Cooperation	Honesty	Punctuality	Tranquility
Coordination	Honor	Quality of work	Trust
Country, love of (patriotism)	Independence	Regularity	Truth
Creativity	Inner peace, calm, quietude	Resourcefulness	Unity
Customer satisfaction	Innovation	Respect for others	Variety
Decisiveness	Integrity	Responsiveness	Wisdom
Delight of being, joy	Justice	Results-oriented	
Democracy	Knowledge	Rule of Law	
Discipline	Leadership	Safety	

Source: http://www.gurusoftware.com/GuruNet/Personal/Topics/Values.htm

For a list of Business values see: http://www.gurusoftware.com/GuruNet/Business/Values.htm

Managing conflict can involve a series of uncomfortable conversations. It can be an incredible growth opportunity where you develop your confidence, skills, and self-esteem.

This worksheet builds on How to have *Difficult Conversations* by adding space to clarify boundaries and to think through work accountabilities and risks for managing the conflict.

Once you embrace healthy conflict as a normal course of doing business, the pressure lessens and you can experience more ease.

Authentic leaders see conflict as a normal part of doing business. Mike Desjardins, CEO, ViRTUS, says that healthy debate in groups needs to be embraced and focused on ideas, while personal conflict is more appropriately dealt with respectfully and in private.

Managing Conflict

— Action Worksheet —

> **Topic Description:**
> *I am so uncomfortable with conflict!*
> *How do I develop my ability to manage conflict in my leadership and my life?*

Use the following worksheet to develop your ability to manage conflict. Remember that having the actual conversation is about thirty percent of the steps required in managing conflict. There are things you can do to support yourself before, during, and after the conversation.

It is focused on situations where you have the time to prepare before you address a conflict. In order to be able to manage conflict in the moment, particularly with people you feel intimidated by, it can be helpful to practice first with lower-risk conversations where you have the time to prepare. Think of this as *advanced conflict management*.

A caveat about managing conflict is that the best way to address it is face-to-face; next is via phone or virtually online. Email is not recommended as the receiver may misinterpret the message and the sender may use it to avoid having the difficult conversation; both can weaken even the strongest of relationships.

Another caveat is that there may be a power differential with the person you are having the conflict with. Remember that good leaders surround themselves with people who give them feedback, particularly when a course correction is required.

Examples are provided for how to say things to the other person, and you are encouraged to find wording that feels comfortable for you. These are meant to be a starting point for you. Remember that you will return to beginner's mind as you learn something new. Compassion for yourself when you may stumble and seeing your practice as progress is essential to continuous learning.

Things to Consider About Managing Conflict:

- You can learn to see conflict as something that may arise from time to time and each situation is a crossroads for a relationship;
- It can be helpful to understand your current automatic or default patterns and beliefs for dealing with it and to become aware of those that may need to shift in order to improve your effectiveness;
- There are different kinds of situations when conflict may arise;
- Minimizing conflict and the amount of energy you expend on it is about clearing annoyances as soon as they occur.

You can learn to see conflict as something that may arise from time to time and each situation is a crossroads for a relationship

Conflict is something that comes up over and over in your life. It is a natural part of every relationship as each of us has a unique personality, different values, and ways of interpreting situations. This means that you aren't always going to agree and you aren't always going to get along. What matters is how you learn to think about and practice managing conflict.

Conflict is often a crossroads in a relationship; it can...

- Strengthen a relationship. For example, *I have a conflict with a peer and through a difficult conversation we come to understand and respect each other more*;
- Weaken it by reducing the trust bank through a huge withdrawal;
- End it if one person is not able to continue the dialogue to keep the relationship going, or when one person intentionally wants to set a boundary to end the relationship.

It can be helpful to understand your current automatic or default patterns and beliefs for dealing with it and to become aware of those that may need to shift in order to improve your effectiveness

The first step to developing your competency at something new is to become aware of what your current mindset is.

How do you think about conflict? For example, *When I become uncomfortable at the first hint of conflict, I shut down and withdraw*, or *when I feel someone is weak because they don't stand up to me, I lose respect for them and use intimidation to get the person to agree*.

What old belief might need to shift for you to be able to engage in conflict more effectively? For example, *I need to change my belief that quiet equals weak*, or *I need to change my belief that if I withdraw, it will go away*.

What assumptions are you making about the person you are in conflict with? Are they causing you to behave differently than if you checked them out and found them to be untrue? Have you checked them out? For example, *I sent an email to a colleague a week ago and haven't received a response – my assumption is they are mad at me*, versus, *I notice that my colleague hasn't responded to me and I need to check out what is going on with him/her before I jump to conclusions*.

There are different kinds of situations when conflict may arise

For some situations, you may be able to avoid them in the moment by checking out your interpretation while with others, you may need to set a boundary where the other person's behaviour is out of alignment with your values. And, with others, you may need to leave a relationship where there is an unworkable incongruence in values.

There are different potential conflict situations that arise in the workplace ranging from:

- Navigating a situation in the moment that could result in conflict based on your automatic patterns and beliefs that create a filter that could distort your interpretation;
- Ongoing conflict minimization through *clearing* annoyances. These are the situations where you get the gift of time to go away and prepare your thoughts in order to have the conversation;
- Situations that are abusive and even illegal such as harassment.

Self-awareness means you are able to have more choice about your reactions. You may be engaging in a conversation and notice you get triggered by something that could cause conflict if it isn't checked out. For example, *My peer makes a comment I get a reaction to and I immediately get defensive. I snap out at him only to find out it wasn't at all what he was intending.*

If you are able to see what you get triggered by, you can begin to notice the uncomfortable feelings arising as you become afraid or angry and you can learn to check it out in the moment. Clarity about your values can support you when you aren't sure if something is acceptable to you or not.

You are able to self-regulate and self-manage if you practice deep belly breathing to remain calm as you check out your interpretation. Often the relationship strengthens as you learn to successfully navigate these. you may also be a role model for a new way of interacting that may be helpful for the other person in the future as well.

Minimizing conflict, and the amount of energy you expend on it is about clearing annoyances as soon as they occur

When you clear *annoyances* on an ongoing basis, you may avoid potential *big issues* that took time to grow out of proportion.

If you clear annoyances, those situations that measure about a two to three out of ten in terms of intensity of frustration, they dissipate and disappear. For example, you talk about them right after they occur, check out assumptions, set boundaries, and anything else that is required. You can prepare your thoughts, get support and role play if needed then, set up a time in a location that is private in order to continue the conversation.

If you let them build up into big issues, those situations that measure about a seven to eight out of ten in terms of intensity, they build up until you may snap and a small thing may become the straw that broke the camel's back instead of it just being another small annoyance that could have been cleared in the moment.

Situations that cross the line into abusive and harassment

There may be situations you encounter when you are totally uncomfortable with how you are being treated/addressed. For example, a bully or a boss who wants to have an affair. This is when a company policy comes in to play and a human resources representative is needed to provide education about what support is available before any situation arises. If one does arise, the representative can provide guidance and support in navigating the situation and the boss, code of conduct advisor or lawyer may not need to be brought in to the situation.

When developing the competence for managing conflict, it can be helpful to first practice clearing annoyances when you have the luxury of time to prepare before practicing managing conflict in the moment.

ACTION STEPS

Practices

Following are the steps you can take to support yourself while managing conflict:
- Before the conversation;
- During the conversation;
- After the conversation.

These steps are meant as a starting point as you develop a way you are comfortable with.

Before the conversation

Reflect on and answer the following questions regarding how you currently deal with conflict:
- How do you think about conflict? Is it something you are used to engaging in? Or, is it something to be avoided at all cost? How do you think the other person feels about conflict?

- Write down both what your intention is for the relationship with the person you are experiencing the conflict with and what your understanding of their intention is. For example, Its a new relationship with someone you need to work together with for several years and you admire their work. Your intention is to maintain a strong relationship with them and work through annoyances as they occur. Or, your intention might be to find a way to work together with mutual respect even if you may not like each other. Or, it might be to end the relationship as there is a difference of values between the two of you.
    - Your intention for this relationship is:

MANAGING CONFLICT

- Your understanding or assumptions about the other person's intention for this relationship — remember you need to check this out:

- Write down what your automatic patterns and beliefs are for managing conflict currently, as well as, what your experience of the other person's. This can also give insight into a misalignment or opportunity for mutual understanding. For example, *When I become uncomfortable at the first hint of conflict I shut down and withdraw*, or *When I feel that a person I'm working with is weak because they don't stand up to me, I lose respect for them and use intimidation to get the person to agree*. If you aren't aware of yours it can be helpful to ask others, friends, family, peers, etc. to understand more about what you don't yet know.
    - Your automatic patterns and beliefs for managing conflict are:

    - The other person's automatic patterns and beliefs for managing conflict currently are:

- Write down one thing that might need to shift for you to be able to engage in conflict more effectively? For example, *I need to change my belief that quiet equals weak. It may simply mean, the other person processes differently than I do*, or *I need to change my belief that if I avoid the situation, it will go away and in order for it to go away more quickly and with much less energy, I may need to practice clearing it as soon as it occurs.*

- Write down the assumptions you are making about the person you are in conflict with. Are they causing you to behave differently than if you checked them out and found them to be untrue? Have you checked them out? For example, *I sent an email to a colleague a week ago and haven't had a response — my assumption is they are mad at me versus I notice that my colleague hasn't responded to me and I need to check out what is going on with him/her before I jump to conclusions.*
  - Assumptions you are making about the person you are in conflict with are:

- What are your values? Write them here, as well as, the company's values, and reflect on whether this situation is in line with them. For example, *I have a value of integrity and I am avoiding conflicts because they are uncomfortable; I may be behaving in a way that is out of alignment with my values.*

MANAGING CONFLICT

- Clarify what your boundary is for this situation, what is acceptable and what is not. Use this simple exercise[44] and the space below to clarify your boundaries.

Inside the Circle

1. **What is acceptable to me in this situation:**

    i.e. respectfully working together with people who inspire me to be better

2. **What is acceptable to me, if I invite it in:**

    i.e. working with a person I have a difficult time interacting with, where I get support to address it and they are willing to work on the relationship

Outside the Circle

What's not acceptable to me in this situation:

i.e. working with a bully and allowing it to affect my confidence and ability to do my job (not trying to address it)

- Draw a circle here and work through what your boundaries are for this situation. Has the situation become something that needs to be outside the circle for you? If so, it may be an *annoyance* you need to have a conversation about to clear it before it becomes a *big issue*.

---

44 Source: The Medicine Cards — learning about spirituality through animals — p 149.

- Clarify what your accountability is and what the risks are of having or not having the conversation. Ask yourself the following:
  - What are the risks of having or not having the conversation? For you? For my team? For the organization? For the community?

  - What is your accountability regarding this situation? For example, with an extreme example to demonstrate the point, *I experienced a situation with a contractor where there was both an incongruence in values, as well as, an act that may be illegal. I have a work accountability and a legal/ethical obligation to have a conversation first with my boss, then either with the person directly or the code of conduct advisor.*

- Set up a time and location with the person and let them know what you'd like to talk about. For example, *I want to check in about something that happened yesterday and it will take about fifteen minutes.* If you talk to them without setting up a time in advance, ask them if now is a good time for them to talk. If not, set up a time that works for both of you. Think about the location choosing somewhere private where you won't be interrupted.
- Prepare your thoughts both about what your objective(s) are for the conversation and about what occurred. Clarify what would be helpful to do differently. Use a specific example of something you experienced rather than hearsay. For example, *I sent you an email and followed up with a phone call about something I needed to get done by yesterday for the board. Because I never heard back from you, I wanted to check out what had happened.*
  - While also adding the objectives the other person, your objectives for this conversation are:

- What you want to have the conversation about; this is the specific thing you experienced that felt out of alignment with your and the company's values:

- Be clear about what it is you would like from the person if it happens again. For example, *What would be helpful for me, if you disagree with the approach or don't have time to respond, is that you call me and we talk about it before the deadline is up.*
    - What would be helpful in the future is:

- Role play; practice prior to having the conversation. It can be helpful to find a person who you trust and who will provide you with support and feedback for the conversation. This needs to be someone who has the courage to tell you how you come across and will provide the feedback in a respectful way. Role play the situation and reflect on your learnings. Adjust your approach as required.
- Maintain your foundational practices the day before and the day of the conversation. If you have foundational practices, these are the days they are most important to keep in place. While they may seem simple, they are actually essential, and will support you in having more capacity for these kinds of conversations:
    - Get enough sleep;
    - Ensure your nutrition supports you, including lots of water;
    - Exercise and meditation can help to calm the nervous system;
    - Any other practices you have in place like journaling, etc.
- Write down the foundational practices you have in place or will need to put in place the day before and day of the conversation. The foundational practices that will support you in having the conversation are:

During the conversation

Bring your notes with you to the meeting with the person and use them if needed. Practice the following during the conversation:

- Share what you'd like to talk to the person about and check in with them about their experience of it. You can let them know that this is difficult for you if you feel it is appropriate;
- Using the Stephen Covey principle seek first to understand, *then to be understood*, ask the other person to clarify their intention for the relationship and then clarify yours as well. Sometimes, clarification of different intentions can resolve conflict as it is just a misunderstanding;
- Again, be specific about what occurred and how you felt as a result;
- Listen with a willingness to be influenced as old beliefs and assumptions may have distorted the experience for you. Other things that may influence you are how tired you were on the day it occurred, how stressed you were, how distracted you were by other things, and how present you were when it happened;
- Ask her/him to say more about what his/her experience was so you deepen your understanding of them. This will give you a moment to regain your composure and stay present in the conversation even if you are nervous. For example, *Can you say more about that?*
- Confirm what you have agreed upon and what the next steps are. Thank them for having the conversation with you.

Reflections

After the conversation

Developing your competency for emotional intelligence and the ability to stay authentic in difficult situations requires continuous learning. What can be helpful is practicing debriefs and reflection in order to clarify your learnings, and adjust your approach for the next time.

Debrief; either meet with the person who supported you in the role play or on your own. Reflect on the situation and answer the following questions:

- What are a few things you learned about yourself and the situation?

- What one thing could you do differently next time as a result of what you learned?

- What two things did you do well? Remember that your inner critic will want to focus on the negative and it can be helpful to balance this out with two things you did well; focus on these as progress:

By seeing difficult conversations as opportunities to learn, you can more readily accept them as they come up. You will grow in your leadership, as well as, support other employees as you do.

Arc of Intense Energy Reflection

Refer to the diagram and description of the Arc of Intense Energy on page 17. Reflect on the topic of this chapter — managing conflict. Answer the following questions in order to understand how the arc is showing up for you:

What is your old, automatic pattern when triggered? For example, *When I become uncomfortable at the first hint of conflict, I shut down and withdraw, or when I feel someone is weak because they don't stand up to me, I lose respect for them and use intimidation to get the person to agree.*

What is a new behaviour, belief or attitude you would like to choose instead? For example, *When I become uncomfortable at the first hint of conflict, I notice my discomfort, realize it is the feeling of fear at confronting it head on, and change my belief that quiet equals weak to quiet means powerfully thoughtful and I set up time to meet with the other person to work through it.*

Practice self-managing through the arc when you are learning about this topic. Begin by paying attention; noticing the energy or discomfort intensifying in the body. As this occurs, practice relaxing your shoulders and belly and deepen and slow your breathing.

This will allow you to feel the emotions as they arise, notice your thoughts and discern if they are aligned with your values or just old, unhelpful messages.

When you learn to discern which is true and right, you will be able to maintain your perspective and choose a response that is appropriate, and authentic, for the situation at hand.

Remember your responses to these two questions. Practice using the new behaviour, belief or attitude as your response when triggered.

After a few weeks of practicing, reflect on what you are learning and how you will adjust your thoughts and behaviours as a result.

Closing Reading

Often there are workable options for solving problems that we will not even see until we become open to the concept of working through problems in relationships, rather than running from the problems.

To negotiate problems, we must be willing to identify the problem, let go of blame... and focus on possible creative solutions. To successfully negotiate and solve problems in relationships, we must have a sense of our bottom line and our boundary issues, so we don't waste time trying to negotiate non-negotiable issues.

We need to learn to identify what both people really want and need and the different possibilities for working that out. We can learn to be flexible without being too flexible. Committed... relationships mean two people are learning to work together through their problems and conflicts in ways that work in both people's best interest.[45]

---

[45] Source: "The Language of Letting Go, Melody Beattie, p 93/94.

As a new leader in particular, one of the normal steps you will go through is the transition from getting results through doing yourself to getting results through others' success.

If you look around at the overwhelmed and frantic leaders who are sometimes only breathing in gasps, you will often find someone who has not yet learned the art of delegating.

Once you realize the work can be done and results improved by letting others take care of the projects they are better at than you are, you can have more ease as you relax into your authenticity and as you focus on the right level of decision-making for your role.

Happy delegating.

Learning to Delegate

— Action Worksheet —

> **Topic Description:**
> *I can do it myself!*
> *How do I delegate and feel ok with it?*

Delegation is a new competency you need to build when learning how to be a leader, as well as, when the level of involvement and amount of doing changes is increased as you take on more accountability.

As employees you are the doers of tasks and are rewarded for this. When you are promoted to a manager you begin the journey of delegation and it can be uncomfortable at first. It's as if you are learning how to ride a bike for the first time and the training wheels come off. You have to learn to support others in being the doers and step back and move out of their way.

I remember when one of my leaders asked to meet with me to talk about a few things. I was accountable for one of his departments and he asked if we could adjust how we worked together as he felt there were areas where I didn't need to be so involved. We took the opportunity to have a good discussion about how we were doing and what was going on for each of us. I realized I was diving too deep into details in some areas where he was meant to be leading and it was challenging for him as he struggled to learn and build relationships with those involved.

When you take on more accountability as a manager, senior manager, or executive you may move out of doing almost completely. You learn how things can get done through the people who report to you and who you work with. Your role shifts from being an individual contributor to one creating the conditions for employees and contractors to be their best. You do this by supporting them in specific ways, as well as, helping them navigate and remove roadblocks, holding them accountable, and recognizing their efforts. It can be helpful to understand a flexible model for leadership such as *Situational Leadership*® by Ken Blanchard. Google the topic and review the model as context for this worksheet.

Use the following worksheet to begin practicing working together more effectively through delegation.

Things to Remember About Delegating:
- It's about letting go of control and being open to trust;
- It's an opportunity to let others shine;
- You can work together more effectively and the end product is better as a result.

Delegating is about letting go of control and being open to trust
- Control is an interesting part of your personality where you hold on so tight in order for things to be comfortable that you sometimes impact others in your path. Saying, *I'd take this road*

instead of the one we're on — why don't you take it in an attempt to get them to drive the way you know is right. Or, *I'll just do that; I know all the steps to take* meaning I can do it better and quicker and getting you involved would mean more work for me. And, *I'll attend the meeting and keep you in the loop* because I want to see what's really going on and build the relationships;
- When you let go of control it can be uncomfortable, particularly if it is new and you are just learning. You can get used to this over time and build your capacity for *not doing* and just being and to see how much less effort it takes as a result. A potential sign that a leader is not delegating enough is when they are overworked and involved in everything. Sound familiar?
- Control and trust — two sides of the same coin? When you have issues of trust it's hard to let go and delegate as well; be honest with yourself about how you feel about your team members. Are there relationships you could strengthen in order to learn to trust each person? Sometimes it requires a leap of faith to be able to delegate. It can be amazing for a person when someone truly believes in them and what they are capable of. How would your team members respond?

It's an opportunity to let others shine
- I remember when I learned to delegate and suddenly great things began to happen and the team members were so much more engaged as a result. And it was so much less effort with more space created in my schedule so I could reflect and stay at a more strategic level in my work;
- When you are in a new role, sometimes you go back to what you are comfortable with — the doing — and in this way you micro-manage and don't provide the opportunity or environment for others to be accountable for what they are capable of; you don't allow them the opportunity to shine;
- Everyone wants to do a good job and be thanked and respected for their contribution. Imagine how frustrating it can be for them when they are asked to be accountable for something and then they aren't given the authority, resources, or autonomy to complete it;
- One of the best bosses I worked with hired me to complete a three-year project. He asked me for my plan and to involve him when I needed help. It was no surprise that he requested that we set up bi-weekly status update meetings and quarterly progress reports. And, *call me when you need me* was his philosophy. Wow, I was one engaged and committed employee as a result;
- And, when I made mistakes, he just asked me what I learned, if I would do it again, and what I could do differently as a result. I remember how his compassion and allowing me to fail helped me to feel safe to learn.

You can work together in a way that there are no surprises and the end product is better as a result
- I worked with another great boss who made sure we met every few months to talk about how we were working together and what we could change to have it be an even better working relationship. We continuously adjusted and created the way we worked with each other where I was encouraged and supported to be my best. And, when it wasn't working, we adjusted it again;
- On my side, I involved him in projects early because I needed to ensure I understood what he wanted specifically. I kept him in the loop and got coaching and asked for support when I needed it; my goal was excellence in results and no surprises for him;

- On his side, he needed to be clear about the objective or project and to ensure that I understood him. He needed to check in on me from time to time, particularly if I was looking stressed or didn't seem myself, and he needed to support me in removing roadblocks when I asked for help;
- It worked really well. So, when I began to work for someone else, I talked to her about this and we adopted a similar practice.

When learning to delegate it can also be helpful to recognize that there are two distinct roles — the supervisor and the employee or contractor.

While the supervisor is accountable for being clear about the task and what is required, the employee or contractor has equal accountability for working effectively with her/his boss or client. For example, the employee or contractor has an accountability to ensure they understand and check with the boss so they are in alignment with the task. By being proactive when challenges occur and communicating as soon as they sense a problem may arise, they are able to ensure there are no surprises for the supervisor during a project.

ACTION STEPS

Practices

The following exercise is written for the person who will be doing the delegating. It outlines six steps within three parts that guides you to be more effective at delegation:

- Part One — When you are entering into a new working relationship with an employee or contractor;
- Part Two — When you are working on a specific task that requires delegation;
- Par Three — On an ongoing basis.

Reflections

Part One: Steps to take while preparing to enter a new working relationship with an employee or contractor

Clarify your self-awareness about delegation by reflecting on the following:

- How do you think about delegation? What are your automatic patterns and beliefs that might impact how you work with others? For example, *Delegating will take too much time and effort — I'll just do it myself.*

Control and trust — two sides of the same coin?

When you have issues of trust it's hard to let go and delegate as well — be honest with yourself about how you feel about your team members. For example, *I trust right away versus it taking time for me to build trust; I am able to let go of control versus holding on very tightly to controlling certain things.*

- Your relationship with trust:

- Your relationship with control:

- What beliefs or automatic patterns might be helpful for you to shift in order to be more effective at delegating? For example, Shift the above belief to the following, *I can get so much more done if I let others help and I can get some things off my plate that I really shouldn't be working on.*

Clarify job accountabilities for yourself and the employee or contractor:

- What you are accountable for:

- What the employee or contractor is accountable for:

In addition to the deliverables for the job, remember to clarify your expectations about her accountability for proactively thinking about how to work with you in order to strengthen the relationship and build trust For example, weekly status updates, regular written reporting, No surprises as a principle, approval of the project plan, structure in place prior to beginning, changes to scope agreed to in advance, communicate errors along with learnings, deciding how to move forward as soon as errors ae made, and others as they arise as you work together.

Clarify how you both like to work together and what your preferences are

Often people forget to have this conversation when they are new at working together. By clarifying and sharing a bit about who you are and how you like to work with others, you can begin to build a foundation of trust, as well as, save time and frustration later.

Spend thirty minutes and reflect on the following to develop your self-awareness around delegating:

Supervisor:

- How you like to work with others. For example, are you a visual learner? Do you prefer text? Or phoning? Do you like face to face meetings, or prefer email? Are you an introvert? An extrovert?

- How you deal with conflict. How you like to be approached if someone needs to have difficult conversation with you, or provide constructive feedback:

- What your values are:

- What motivates you:

- Any other information that could be helpful for you to share with the employee or contractor in order for him/her to feel comfortable and work effectively together with you:

Employee/Contractor:
- How _____ (name of the employee or contractor) likes to work with you. You need to ask and maybe support them in becoming aware of their preferences:

- How he/she likes to work with others. Is she a visual learner? Prefers text? Or phoning? Likes to interact best via face to face meetings, email, other? Introvert? Extrovert?

- How he/she deals with conflict? How he/she likes to be approached if I need to have difficult conversation with him/her? Or constructive feedback?

- What are him/her values?

- What motivates him/her?

Exercise

Part Two: Steps to take while preparing when you are overwhelmed or when you are working on a specific task that requires delegation

Prepare yourself for delegating when it's new to you; identify the task to be delegated

Complete the following exercise if you are new to delegating or whenever you are feeling overwhelmed by the volume of work, or when you notice you are resisting delegating to your employees.

Make a list with three columns. In the first, list everything you are accountable for. In the second, list the deadlines. And, in the third, list the names of people who can complete each task. Ask yourself if there are tasks where you don't need to be involved or where you need to delegate and provide support and direction to a team member who is actually accountable. Complete the list in a way that allows you to give up at least ten percent of the tasks or more if it feels appropriate.

Task:	Deadline:	Who can do this if not me:

Assess the level of development and leadership style required for this situation or task

Assess where the person is on the learning curve and what the appropriate leadership style is for you to use in this situation. Reflect on what you have learned in your research on *Situational Leadership*® model by Ken Blanchard, as you work through the following.

- **Developmental level:**
  Disillusioned learner; D2 — a high performer who is on a new project and is overwhelmed. On this task, she has low levels of both competence and commitment.

- **Leadership style required:**
  Coaching/Selling; S2 — support and provide direction if needed as this person may not know how to do something and may need encouragement as they are frustrated.

  The employee or contractor's developmental level is:

  The appropriate leadership style for me to use is:

  Have the conversation with them using the appropriate leadership style.

  Ask them to keep you in the loop, agree on next steps and timelines, and remind them to ask for help when needed. They have an accountability for being aware of where they are on the learning curve and to ask for what they need.

  Check in on them from time to time to see how they is doing.

Practices

Part Three: Steps to practice on an ongoing basis as support for working more effectively together through appropriate delegation

Take time to reflect each month on how the relationship is working

Notice how it feels to know that the tasks are getting done and you don't have to be the person to do them.

Check in with the employee or contractor on a quarterly basis to assess how the working relationship is going for her and what can be done to work even more effectively together now that you are getting to know each other.

- What can you do differently as a result of what you are learning?

- How is the relationship working for you? Are there things we can do differently so you feel more comfortable and we work together more effectively? For example, set up weekly meetings, instead of monthly, for ten minutes to check in to ensure we are on the same page for the project at this stage of progress and identify any risks that you need to be aware of.

- How is the relationship working for the employee or contractor? Are there things that she would like us to do differently to support her in feeling more comfortable and working together more effectively?

- What one thing are we doing well together that we can recognize and celebrate? In order to balance the thoughts of the inner critic, it can be helpful to end with something that is working well. If not, or we may focus on the challenges instead.

Arc of Intense Energy Reflection

Refer to the diagram and description of the Arc of Intense Energy on page 17. Reflect on the topic of this chapter — learning to delegate. Answer the following questions in order to understand how the arc is showing up for you:

What is your old, automatic pattern when triggered? For example, *When I notice resentment when I am doing the work that my team should be doing, I keep on doing it because they won't get it right.*

What is a new behaviour, belief or attitude you would like to choose instead? For example, *When I notice resentment when I am doing the work that my team should be doing, I notice my overwhelm, realizing it is my signal to delegate. I transfer accountability to the appropriate team member and coach them to get it done to the expected standard, within the time allotted.*

Practice self-managing through the arc when you are learning about this topic. Begin by paying attention; noticing the energy or discomfort intensifying in the body. As this occurs, practice relaxing your shoulders and belly and deepen and slow your breathing.

This will allow you to feel the emotions as they arise, notice your thoughts and discern if they are aligned with your values or just old, unhelpful messages.

When you learn to discern which is true and right, you will be able to maintain your perspective and choose a response that is appropriate, and authentic, for the situation at hand.

Remember your responses to these two questions. Practice using the new behaviour, belief or attitude as your response when triggered.

After a few weeks of practicing, reflect on what you are learning and how you will adjust your thoughts and behaviours as a result.

Closing Reading

The great leaders are like the best conductors —
they reach beyond the notes to reach the magic in the players.
~ Blaine Lee[46]

---

46 http://humanresources.about.com/od/workrelationships/a/quotes_empower.htm

> I love giving feedback. It is such an important conversation to have and yet one that leaders rarely undertake.
>
> Often feedback is negative and is difficult to both give and to receive.
>
> Often the positive feedback is not given.
>
> This worksheet takes an authentic approach to feedback in that it focuses first on building awareness about the impacts and discomfort of receiving feedback. Once embraced and understood, this then supports providing feedback with a level of empathy and respect that is grounded in a way that it would not have been otherwise.

Receiving and Giving Feedback

— Action Worksheet —

> **Topic Description:**
> *I don't know how or what to say!*
> *How can I give feedback that is meaningful and effective when it feels uncomfortable?*

Feedback is one of the quickest and easiest ways for you to grow. It can also be one of the most difficult things to ask for. Many people have a strong inner critic. Your mind may get triggered by feedback as it thinks you are being attacked. Sometimes feedback is difficult to hear because it reveals a quality about you that you aren't happy about. And sometimes feedback is difficult to hear because it is positive and highlights a strength — that can be uncomfortable to hear as well; especially if you aren't used to hearing the positives.

Things to Remember About Feedback:
- It can be profoundly helpful and remembered for years;
- It is one of the quickest ways to grow;
- It can be uncomfortable to hear — either positively or constructively;
- There are five types of feedback to consider;
- It is helpful to get used to receiving it in order to provide it effectively to others.

Beginning with the last point, *it is helpful to get used to receiving feedback in order to provide it effectively to others* please search online and watch the TEDx video called *How to use others' feedback to learn and grow* by Sheila Heen, Author of *Difficult Conversations* and professor at Harvard Business School. The link is shown here as well: https://www.youtube.com/watch?reload=9&v=FQNbaKkYk_Q

- Reflect on three things you learned from the video about the importance of proactively and regularly seeking out feedback:

- Reflect on how you feel when you receive feedback. Write what your awareness is here:

- Reflect on how you feel when giving feedback. Is it something you embrace or avoid? What gets in your way?

- What awareness do you have of your automatic pattern when triggered by feedback?

- Ideally, how would you like to feel? How would you like to respond?

When you understand your own patterns of thought and behaviour when seeking out and receiving feedback, it helps to remind yourself what others go through when you provide it to them. By considering their state of mind and level of anxiety, you can begin to frame the feedback in a way that is authentic, respectful, and specific. By doing this, you increase the chances of the person being able to receive the feedback while maintaining their self-esteem and self-respect. And through this, they will grow. And as they grow stronger, so will the team.

Now, let's look at different types of feedback and how we can begin to practice providing it proactively to others.

Types of feedback

There are different situations where feedback is helpful, as well as, different ways of asking and providing it.

Positive and Quick — Specific feedback about something you observed that was done very well. Use this the majority of the time;

Constructive and Quick — Specific feedback about something you observed that could have been done more effectively. If it's vague, the person can get confused and won't have anything specific to work on. It's frustrating and leaves the person going below the line as they don't have enough information to act on;

Detailed Feedback about a task — Detailed feedback that is both positive and constructive about each of the steps taken to complete a task. As the person is completing the task, delivering a presentation, fixing a machine, creating a board member briefing, developing a schedule or work plan, provide two to three specific insights for every stage of the task on what they did well and what they could have done differently;

Detailed Debrief after a project — Doing a detailed debrief that is both positive and constructive about how a project was completed, at main milestones, as well as, once completed. Learnings are captured and team members get closure as it is celebrated and finalized;

Detailed Feedback, both positive and constructive about performance over time — Detailed Feedback about performance over time is usually done as part of annual performance-management cycle. It can be done as a 360 Review if received from several people around the person.

Here are formats and examples for each, as well as, a self-reflection for you to begin practicing giving others feedback.

Positive and Quick

May I share some feedback with you?

I noticed X (the facts) or I heard you say X (what they said).

That was very effective in that you did Y (the specifics of what they did) as it meant that (describe the positive impact it had).

Thank you for X (doing that).

Example:

In the meeting, you did a great job of fielding a controversial question from Bob who was angry about the project. You stayed calm and respectful, answered it directly and clearly with the facts, and then checked with him to see if he had any other questions about it.

Bob calmed down, thanked you, and we were able to move on to the next part of the meeting. The team look to you as a role model and you showed them how to respond effectively, so thank you.

Self-Reflection

Prepare your thoughts using the following model, for how you would provide your colleague with positive feedback that is specific and can be communicated quite quickly, within five minutes.

May I share some feedback with you?

I noticed X (the facts) or I heard you say X (what they said).

That was very effective in that you did Y (the specifics of what they did) as it meant that (describe the positive impact it had).

Thank you for X (doing that).

RECEIVING AND GIVING FEEDBACK

Constructive and Quick

May I share some feedback with you?

I noticed X (the facts) or I heard you say X (what they said).

What I am having difficulty with was Y (the specifics of what they did).

What would be helpful going forward is if you could do Z. (how they could do it differently).

Example:

In the meeting, I heard you say "The subcontractor, Sherry, is an idiot and we should get rid of her". What I'm having difficulty with is you are an influencer and when you speak disrespectfully about someone in front of others, they think this is the right way to do it and it's acceptable, so they can do it too.

What would be helpful in the future is if you speak directly to the subcontractor and provide specific feedback in private when you are having an issue with them. Also, it would be helpful to coach others to use this approach as well.

Self-Reflection

Prepare your thoughts, using the following model, for how you would provide someone at work with constructive feedback that is specific and can be communicated quite quickly (within five minutes).

May I share some feedback with you?

I noticed X (the facts) or I heard you say X (what they said).

What I am having difficulty with was Y (the specifics of what they did).

What would be helpful going forward is if you could do Z. (how they could do it differently).

Detailed Feedback about a task

This is used when a person wants to understand specifically how they can be more effective at a task that has several steps like completing a mechanical fix of a machine, presenting to the board, facilitating a department meeting, and they may have done things well, but could tweak how they do other things during several steps of the task.

Section/Task:	Feedback:
Section One	Great: write down specific details of the section and what they did well. Could have done differently: write down specific details of the section and what and how they could do it differently.
Section Two	Great: write down specific details of the section and what they did well. Could have done differently: write down specific details of the section and what and how they could do it differently.
Section Three	Great: write down specific details of the section and what they did well. Could have done differently: write down specific details of the section and what and how they could do it differently.

Example:

Section/Task:	Feedback:
Preparation before the department meeting	Great: *you communicated a week in advance what the agenda and purpose of the meeting were.* Could have done differently: *you provided the background documents and the specific questions you wanted participants to consider.*
Facilitating the department meeting	Great: *you invited your direct reports to present on each of their areas and then you thanked them for their participation.* Could have done differently: *you invited the quieter team members to participate and we didn't hear from them a lot and I know they have valuable things to say. Maybe do a roundtable next time so we hear from everyone.*
Follow up	Great: *you had the names and accountabilities for tasks sent out to the team within three days of the meeting.* Could have done differently: *you asked the people accountable for next steps to be ready to provide an update in the next team meeting.*

Detailed Debrief after a project

Have a conversation after a project is completed and debrief it with the team. Make it about the processes and not about the individuals. Feedback for individuals should be done in private and with them directly.

Discuss each of the following:

What went well?

What could have been done differently?

Anything else we want to apply next time?

Example:

What went well?

We partnered with the client right from the start so they were engaged and involved in all big decisions.

We proactively let the client know when we were going to be out of scope so they didn't have any surprises about the overrun and they made the decision to spend the extra funds.

What could have been done differently?

Worked with the subcontractors to forecast any out of scope, and longer time issues proactively each week. Cost and time overruns are our biggest risk.

Anything else we want to apply next time?

Have a weekly status update meeting where we focus on what we are doing well and what problems might be occurring this week. Involve the mechanics and the machine operators in these meetings.

Detailed Feedback about performance over time. This can be a 360 Review if received from several people

Detailed Feedback about performance over time is usually done as part of annual performance-management cycle.

Understand the business objectives and goal for performance. For example, what an excellent job looks like from the company's perspective. Share your feedback in the context of this understanding. If a person seeks feedback from their boss, peers, and those who report directly to them, this is considered a 360 Review which requires getting feedback from all those around them.

Strengths: share five things the person did well. These are five things you have already provided them with specific feedback about during the year and are highlights of their successes. No Surprises is a good philosophy so the person knows what they are walking into when they participate in this kind of a conversation.

Opportunities for Development: share two things the person could do differently. Again, these have already been discussed at the time they occurred.

Goals for the future: understand their personal and professional goals and provide guidance on one to two things they can learn or develop in order to more forward toward their long-term goals.

There isn't an example for this one as it's so unique to each role and each person.

Arc of Intense Energy Reflection

Refer to the diagram and description of the Arc of Intense Energy on page 17. Reflect on the topic of this chapter — receiving and giving feedback. Answer the following questions in order to understand how the arc is showing up for you:

What is your old, automatic pattern when triggered? For example, *When I am triggered by my boss asking me if he can give me some feedback, I notice fear arising and my inner critic saying "you must have done something wrong"*.

What is a new behaviour, belief or attitude you would like to choose instead? For example, *When I am triggered by my boss asking me if he can give me some feedback, I notice fear arising and my inner critic saying "you must have done something wrong". I deepen my breathing and shift my thoughts. I get curious about the feedback reminding myself it could be something positive I have done.*

Practice self-managing through the arc when you are learning about this topic. Begin by paying attention; noticing the energy or discomfort intensifying in the body. As this occurs, practice relaxing your shoulders and belly and deepen and slow your breathing.

This will allow you to feel the emotions as they arise, notice your thoughts and discern if they are aligned with your values or just old, unhelpful messages.

When you learn to discern which is true and right, you will be able to maintain your perspective and choose a response that is appropriate, and authentic, for the situation at hand.

Remember your responses to these two questions. Practice using the new behaviour, belief or attitude as your response when triggered.

After a few weeks of practicing, reflect on what you are learning and how you will adjust your thoughts and behaviours as a result.

Closing Reading:

We feel safe around direct, honest people. They speak their minds, and we know where we stand with them.

(We may believe that) indirect people, people who are afraid to say who they are, what they want, and what they're feeling, cannot be trusted.

They will somehow act out their truth even though they do not speak it.

And it may catch everyone by surprise.

Directness saves time and energy. It removes us as victims. It dispenses with martyrdom and games. It helps us own our power.

It creates respectful relationships.

It feels safe to be around direct, honest people.

Be one.[47]

---

[47] Directness, June 1st, from "The Language of Letting Go", Melody Beattie, 1990, p 148.

This is a new topic that has yet to be shared publicly.

I wrote it as I was asked to speak at a women's network gathering and at the last moment was unable to.

The idea that joy is our natural state comes from both the work of Eckhart Tolle and Michael A. Singer. And, I am sure there are many others.

It gave me a different lens through which to see the world as an authentic leader if I could return over and over to this state of being and see the others, anger and fear, as temporary ones that I could choose to move through and let go of.

Cultivating Joy at Work

— Action Worksheet —

Topic Description:
I want to experience joy and ease at work!
How do I cultivate joy when I am so busy and overwhelmed at work?

You spend a lot of time at work in your life. Sometimes it can feel overwhelming with the sheer volume of work, as well as, the amount of change and the challenges dealing with peers, direct reports, clients, and others. Cultivating joy while working creates an environment where you and your team can thrive. It creates a right brain state from a neuroscience perspective for effective learning and performance. It also supports resiliency and it helps you keep perspective when things get busy or tough.

The big question is, *Does cultivating joy at work come from what you do or is it a state of being?*

Use the following worksheet to begin practicing learning how to cultivate joy more of the time in order to support your leadership and your life. Remember that when something is challenging you at work or at home, it will show up in your life in different ways until you *wake up* to it and make a shift in how you think about it, and then change your habits and behaviours.

Things to consider when learning how to cultivate joy:

- Joy is your natural state. When you are fully present and being your authentic self, joy becomes your default;
- Joy is a choice. You can choose to practice presence for more joy in every moment;
- It is helpful to know what joy feels like and to have a vocabulary for describing it;
- Cultivating joy requires practice.

Joy is your natural state. When you are present and being your authentic self, joy becomes your default

In Eckhart Tolle's book, *A new Earth — Awakening to your Life's Purpose*, he says that as humans, our inner purpose as a species is to evolve beyond thought because the thinking or egoic mind is often unhelpful and creates unnecessary stress, and our outer purpose is to see how that manifests in our lives on an ongoing basis as we evolve internally.

In his book, *The Untethered Soul*, and his online course, *Living from a Place of Surrender*, Michael A. Singer describes our true self as a state of ecstatic joy that arises once we remember *who we truly are* — being aware of our thoughts and emotions and when we know *how to let go of ego* — the largely negative, unhelpful, and endless stream of thoughts that provides our sense of self or identity. We need to reach this awareness in order to experience complete presence and the joy of each precious moment.

Being your authentic self means *being genuine and a role model for moral behavior* and this way of being occurs when you begin a journey to awaken. It involves remembering who you are as your best or authentic self which is often forgotten as you go through life and may be hidden away underneath layers of personality, ego or identity — one or two of which are incredibly unhelpful, like the inner critical voice that may keep you from living your potential.

Joy is a choice. You can choose to practice presence for more joy in every moment

The way the mind works is that you have an endless stream of thoughts. When you begin to practice awareness of them you notice they are either positive or negative and that when unaware, your current default is that they are largely negative and often unhelpful.

With awareness and practicing presence for an open heart, you experience each moment as the world unfolds and you either resist it or allow it to impress upon you and touch your soul.

You also realize that in every moment you have a choice, you can either listen to the thoughts and be guided by them, or you can rise up above the thoughts and practice relaxing in order to let them go and be guided by a deep inner knowing that arises through complete presence.

Grumpy or grateful, angry or joyful — in every moment it's your choice.

The video from Conscious Leadership called *Location, Location, Location*, affectionately known as the *Above and Below the Line* video, gives a great model for understanding how the mind works.

It is helpful to know what joy feels like and to have a vocabulary for describing it

In order to experience and express joy, it is helpful to practice awareness of what it feels like. This may sound easier than it actually is.

In addition, developing the language to express joy, gives you more words to articulate the subtleties of the emotional experience.

ACTION STEPS

Reflections and Practices

Cultivating joy requires practice. Here are a few for you:

- A simple practice to cultivate joy is to notice when you are being negative and to reframe it to a positive. Notice when you are below the line and make a choice to move back above the line. One place to practice is when you are waiting for someone. Notice if your mind says something like, *I hate waiting*, or *What a waste of my time*. Notice the emotion this brings up. It could be frustration or anger. Reframe it to something more positive like, *I am so grateful to have a moment to breathe — it's been such a busy week*.

- Write down a negative thought that arises when you are waiting:

- Write down how you can reframe this thought to something more positive:

- Notice how each thought feels differently.
- Notice how your state of being, either positive or negative, impacts the quality of the interaction with the person you are meeting with.
• If you would like to dive deeper into cultivating joy, it is helpful to understand what occurs physiologically when you are triggered by a person or situation and you are about to take on your stress pattern of fight, flight or freeze.
    - A simple reflection is to practice presence and re-center when you are not in your natural state of ease or joy. Notice the point at which your mind is triggered. Once you have this awareness, override the thought that is triggering you and *relax and release*.[48]
    - Relax the belly, shoulders, and the forehead, and release the thought that triggered you. The caveat is to listen to the thought if an issue of physical safety arises.

---
[48] Living from a Place of Surrender, Michael A. Singer, Online Course, Session 7.

Arc of Intense Energy Reflection

Refer to the diagram and description of the Arc of Intense Energy on page 17. Reflect on the topic of this chapter — cultivating joy at work. Answer the following questions in order to understand how the arc is showing up for you:

What is your old, automatic pattern when triggered? For example, *When I am triggered by the new requests for work I am expected to add to my plate when I am already working nights and weekends, I notice anxiety and resentment arising and I get depressed and shut down.*

What is a new behaviour, belief or attitude you would like to choose instead? For example, *When I am triggered by the new requests for work I am expected to add to my plate when I am already working nights and weekends, I notice anxiety and resentment arising. I realize I haven't had lunch or a break yet and it's already 3:00 in the afternoon. I take a break, have a 15 min walk and eat lunch for 30 min. I have a full glass of water instead of coffee. I remind myself that in each moment I have a choice in how I respond to the situation and I meet with my boss to work through priorities and share my experience of overwhelm.*

Practice self-managing through the arc when you are learning about this topic. Begin by paying attention; noticing the energy or discomfort intensifying in the body. As this occurs, practice relaxing your shoulders and belly and deepen and slow your breathing.

This will allow you to feel the emotions as they arise, notice your thoughts and discern if they are aligned with your values or just old, unhelpful messages.

When you learn to discern which is true and right, you will be able to maintain your perspective and choose a response that is appropriate, and authentic, for the situation at hand.

Remember your responses to these two questions. Practice using the new behaviour, belief or attitude as your response when triggered.

After a few weeks of practicing, reflect on what you are learning and how you will adjust your thoughts and behaviours as a result.

Resources

Books:

A New Earth — Awaken to your Life's Purpose, Eckhart Tolle

The Untethered Soul, Michael A. Singer

Online Course:

Living from a Place of Surrender, Michael A. Singer

Closing Readings

External Cultivation of Joy — What you are doing:

Do something fun today.

If you are relaxing, let yourself relax, without guilt, without worrying about the work that is undone.

If you're with loved ones, let yourself love them, and them love you.

Let yourself feel close.

Let yourself enjoy your work, for that can be pleasurable too.

If you're doing something fun, let yourself enjoy it. What would feel good?

What would you enjoy? Is there a positive pleasure available? Indulge.

Today, I will do something fun, something I enjoy, something just for me.

I will take responsibility for making myself feel good.

Adapted from: The Language of Letting Go, Melody Beattie, Enjoying Life — November 6th, p 322, © 1990.

Internal Cultivation of Joy — Your state of being — consciousness / authenticity:

…what is the relationship between something that you do and the state of joy?

You will enjoy any activity in which you are fully present, any activity that is not just a means to an end. It isn't the action you perform that you really enjoy, but the deep sense of aliveness that flows into it. That aliveness is one with who you are.

This means that when you enjoy doing something, you are really experiencing the joy of Being in its dynamic aspect. That's why anything you enjoy doing connects you with the power behind all creation.[49]

Eckhart Tolle, A New Earth, p299. © 2005.

---

49 Eckhart Tolle, A New Earth, p299. © 2005.

It has been helpful over the years to see relationship-building in order to promote business in a more positive light than the old language of networking or business development.

A more authentic approach is one where relationship-building creates a win-win outcome and better results by taking on a positive tone where relationships are nourished over time.

If it is done without attachment to outcomes, the results may be as simple as meeting a new friend. If there is a natural connection, then the possibilities are endless.

This topic was written for a Women's Network evening where the focus was on a values-centered authentic approach versus the more traditional one of networking.

We are the *walk-betweeners*, those who walk between the old traditional ways of doing business and leading others and the new ones who are focused on consciousnesses and integrity. Cultivate your way, not necessarily the one that others espouse.

Building Relationships Authentically

— Action Worksheet —

> **Topic Description:**
> *Networking often feels phony for me!*
> *How can I connect with others in a genuine way while building my business?*

Networking — relationship-building with a purpose — is essential for business and for life. In order to have exceptional relationship-building skills, it is helpful to have a simple model for authentic networking.

Authentic Networking

Steps Toward Building Relationships in a Way that is Authentic:

- Finding the right mindset — Reframing networking to create ease and joy;
- Preparing for the meeting — Discovering your values, what your purpose for the meeting is, and what questions you will ask;
- Practicing with someone — Trying it out, learning from the experience, and applying your learnings to the next meeting.

Finding the right mindset

Complete the following self-reflection to understand how you think about networking, what supports you, and what may be getting in your way.

- How do you currently think about networking? Is it something you are excited by? Intimidated by? For example, *I'm afraid of networking as I will have to be aggressive and it will be uncomfortable.*

- What are two strengths that support you to be an effective networker? For example, *I like to help others succeed and I'm a good listener*.

- What self-limiting beliefs do you have about networking that may get in your way? For example, *I'm an introvert and am too shy to network*.

- How can you positively reframe networking so it opens up different possibilities and you can experience ease and enjoyment? For example, *Relationship-building is like planting a garden — it takes planting a lot of seeds for some to germinate. Some take hold right away, some after a bit of time, and some never will. Gardens also take long-term nurturing in good weather and bad, and the result is a lifetime of beauty and pleasure.*
Write down how you think about networking, positively, so it sets the tone for you going forward:

Prepare for the meeting

Preparation includes three parts. The first requires gaining personal clarity about an approach that aligns with your values. The second entails clarifying the purpose and setting an intention, and the third involves preparing questions you will use when you are at the networking event.

Gaining personal clarity

- Values are underlying beliefs about what is right for you and your life. They provide guidance for how you can approach your life, your leadership, and even networking. Review the list of Values words[50] on the next page and select up to ten that you resonate with. Add additional words if yours are missing from this list.
  Your values are: For example, Family/Relationships, Integrity/Authenticity, Wellness, In-service, Abundance, Ease/Savoring/Joy

- Reflect on how you could approach networking in a way that is aligned with your values. Write down three things you can do to lead with your values when you network. For example, *I can use an approach that feels right for me like meeting one to two people at an event. I can connect them to someone else or provide a value-added resource for them as a follow-up. I enjoy the relationship without attachment — they may be my next best friend who I just haven't met yet.*

---

50 Source: http://www.gurusoftware.com/GuruNet/Personal/Topics/Values.htm

Values Words — Common Personal Values:

Accomplishment, Success	Discovery	Love, Romance	Satisfying others
Accountability	Ease of Use	Loyalty	Security
Accuracy	Efficiency	Maximum utilization (of time, resources)	Self-givingness
Adventure	Equality	Meaning	Self-reliance
All for one & one for all	Excellence	Merit	Simplicity
Beauty	Fairness	Money	Skill
Calm, quietude, peace	Faith	Openness	Speed
Challenge	Family	Peace, Non-violence	Spirit in life (using)
Change	Family feeling	Perfection (e.g. of details)	Stability
Cleanliness, orderliness	Flair	Personal Growth	Standardization
Collaboration	Freedom	Pleasure	Status
Commitment	Friendship	Positive attitude	Strength
Communication	Fun	Power	Succeed; A will to-
Community	Global view	Practicality	Success, Achievement
Competence	Good will	Preservation	Systemization
Competition	Goodness	Privacy	Teamwork
Concern for others	Gratitude	Problem Solving	Timeliness
Content over form	Hard work	Progress	Tolerance
Continuous improvement	Harmony	Prosperity, Wealth	Tradition

Cooperation	Honesty	Punctuality	Tranquility
Coordination	Honor	Quality of work	Trust
Country, love of (patriotism)	Independence	Regularity	Truth
Creativity	Inner peace, calm, quietude	Resourcefulness	Unity
Customer satisfaction	Innovation	Respect for others	Variety
Decisiveness	Integrity	Responsiveness	Wisdom
Delight of being, joy	Justice	Results-oriented	
Democracy	Knowledge	Rule of Law	
Discipline	Leadership	Safety	

Source: http://www.gurusoftware.com/GuruNet/Personal/Topics/Values.htm

For a list of Business values see: http://www.gurusoftware.com/GuruNet/Business/Values.htm

Clarifying the purpose and setting an intention

- Prepare to meet and network with one of the other participants today
- Determine your Purpose for Networking at this event and write it here: For example, *My purpose is to get to know other great women in the energy industry*.

- Set an Intention, one that frames the experience you want to have in a positive way: For example, *I am looking forward to getting to know some amazing women and to being inspired as I start to know them better*.

- Remember their names by finding your way to remember; repeating it back, checking the spelling, remembering a feature about the person that reminds you of their name, use it two times in the conversation.

Preparing Questions

- Seek first to understand by having three questions in your mind that you can ask them. For example, *What do you do? Where are you from? Can you tell me more about your work? What is it that you love about that?*
Questions you can ask are:

Practice being present and actively listening. Repeat back your understanding and ask further questions to deepen the conversation.

Next, share about yourself at the level you are comfortable with. For example, Who you are, What you do.

Once you have an understanding of who they are and you have made a connection, offer one thing you can do to support them. For example, send them an article or video about a topic they told you about or provide a solution to a challenge they have.

Follow up with the support, article, etc., you offered and do what you said you would do and when you promised it by. In addition, follow up to reconnect and continue building the relationship.

ACTION STEPS

Practices
Now try it out. Have a conversation with someone you haven't spoken to yet today. Then switch and get to know one other person as well. Once you have completed meeting two people, reflect on what you learned:

Reflections
- How did it go? Rate out of ten:

- What two things did you do well?

- What one thing could you have done differently?

Practice your new skill:

- Like any new skill, practice means progress;
- Decide on three networking events you will attend in the next two months;
- Use this Action Worksheet, and the three-step model to develop your approach, clarify your purpose, set an intention, prepare for the event, and enjoy the process;
- Attend the events and practice your skills. Pay attention to when you are enjoying yourself during the evening and what feels aligned with your values;
- Meet within the next month with your partner today to share learnings with each other about what worked well and what you will do differently the next time.

Arc of Intense Energy Reflection

Refer to the diagram and description of the Arc of Intense Energy on page 17. Reflect on the topic of this chapter — building relationships authentically. Answer the following questions in order to understand how the arc is showing up for you:

What is your old, automatic pattern when triggered? For example, *When I am triggered by the need to attend a networking event with many people I don't know, I notice anxiety arising and I resist and cancel at the last minute.*

What is a new behaviour, belief or attitude you would like to choose instead? For example, *When I am triggered by the need to attend a networking event with many people I don't know, I notice anxiety arising and I remind myself that as an introvert I can build relationships in a way that works for me. I deepen and slow my breathing and set an intention to "meet 1-2 people and to spend the entire evening getting to know them" rather than having to pass my card out to 20 or more.*

Practice self-managing through the arc when you are learning about this topic. Begin by paying attention; noticing the energy or discomfort intensifying in the body. As this occurs, practice relaxing your shoulders and belly and deepen and slow your breathing.

This will allow you to feel the emotions as they arise, notice your thoughts and discern if they are aligned with your values or just old, unhelpful messages.

When you learn to discern which is true and right, you will be able to maintain your perspective and choose a response that is appropriate, and authentic, for the situation at hand.

Remember your responses to these two questions. Practice using the new behaviour, belief or attitude as your response when triggered.

After a few weeks of practicing, reflect on what you are learning and how you will adjust your thoughts and behaviours as a result.

Closing Reading:

Life is a Gentle Teacher. She will keep repeating the lesson until we learn. It is okay to become frustrated. Confused. Angry. Sometimes it is okay to despair. Then, it is okay to walk away and allow the breakthrough to come.

It shall.[51]

---

51 Learning New Behaviours, May 9 from "The Language of Letting Go", Melody Beattie, 1990, p 129.

In organizations, leaders spend a LOT of time in meetings. Some of these gatherings are so memorable in a good way that you remember them for many years... and some are not.

While you may expect the leader or facilitator of a meeting to be responsible for making the most of your precious time, there is another role to consider which is yours as the self-responsible participant.

With authenticity and awareness, self-responsibility means that you hold yourself accountable for the success of the meeting, as well as, the host. You ask yourself how you can contribute to its effectiveness and how can you support both the organizer and other participants.

Imagine the difference in the quality of interactions, not to mention the results, if each participant practiced authenticity when preparing for, attending, and following up after each meeting.

Having Effective Meetings

— Action Worksheet —

> **Topic Description:**
> *I'm feeling overwhelmed!*
> *How do I conduct effective meetings when there seems to be so many of them?*

What is an Effective Meeting?

Whether face-to-face, via conference call or using webcam technology, leaders spend a lot of their working hours in meetings. Creating these opportunities in groups are essential to setting direction, getting things done, inspiring the team, and communicating any host of topics that require discussion and engagement.

What you may not always consider is your role in them. How would meetings change if all participants felt one hundred percent responsible for a successful outcome?

There are at least two main roles in meetings being the meeting owner and the participant. While the meeting owner may understand they are responsible for a successful meeting, the participant doesn't always remember that they play an integral role in it as well.

Learnings to Consider for an Effective Meeting Considering the Meeting Participant's Role:
- Be discerning — understand the objective of the meeting in advance and whether you are the right person to be involved. Sometimes, you get requests to participate when you aren't the person accountable for the topic and don't have a clear part to play in the decision making. Ask for the agenda in advance and what the expectation is for how you can contribute to ensure this is a successful meeting;
- Be prepared — as a participant, review materials, and formulate questions and opinions in advance of the meeting. Talk to others attending to understand any points of contention and to share your ideas if it would be helpful for them to be run by others in advance;
- Be accountable — at the end of each meeting, take the initiative to clarify what the outcomes are, who is responsible for completion of any tasks that come out of it, as well as, what deadlines are required. Clarify anything you aren't quite sure about. If you go away and work on something that is headed in the wrong direction, you'll waste both your time and others. Do your part on time and ensure you communicate with those you promised to touch base with after the meeting is complete;
- Be authentic — notice when your mind thinks *don't say that* for whatever reason your mind has at that moment, and override the inner critical voice in the moment. It may stop you from saying exactly what is needed in the moment to change the course of the conversation. While being aware of your tone, speak your truth, particularly when uncomfortable.

Learnings to Consider for an Effective Meeting Considering with the Meeting Owner's Role:

- Be authentic — your mood and energy set the tone for the meeting. Think of each meeting as an opportunity to instill the culture and values of the organization. Start with a simple check-in to allow everyone to bring their full selves into the room in advance of the topic. This can even be a quick roundtable of one-word per participant if the meeting is on a tight timeline;
- Be inclusive — having both extroverts and introverts in a meeting, send materials out in advance with clear request for what is required of the participants. Be sure you haven't missed any important context because you expect them to just know it and they actually may not. Let them know clearly what the objective of the meeting is;
- Be prepared — as the host, keep the meeting on time, manage participation so the quiet ones participate as much as the more talkative. For example, do a roundtable, at a break, respectfully ask a participant who is dominating the meeting to leave space for others to weigh in and follow up where needed;
- Be clear — one of the biggest opportunities for effective meetings is to transfer accountability to the person who will be taking on the work assigned as a result of a meeting. Ask participants to clarify their understanding of the task, and the timing and expectations for quality. If you don't transfer accountability, in their eyes as well as yours, you may have different expectations for what the next steps are.

What an effective meeting looks like

In order to have effective meetings it is helpful to define what one looks like. As a group, reflect on the following and record what qualifies as both effective and ineffective for your organization:

- What are three attributes of an effective meeting?

- What one thing occurs to make a meeting ineffective?

- What does an effective meeting feel like?

- Who is your role model for hosting the most effective meetings? Who is your role model as a participant? What three leadership qualities do each of them bring into meetings?

Meeting participant; questions and practices for effective meetings

Review the following questions and practices to improve the effectiveness of meetings when your role is as a participant.

Be discerning
- What is the objective of this meeting? What questions do you need to ask, and of who in order to be clear?

- Are you the right person to be a participant? Are the right people invited? If not, who do you need to speak with to ensure they are?

- What is the agenda for the meeting and how long do we have? Are there any requested changes to ensure the meeting is a success?

- What is your role as a participant if you accept one hundred percent responsibility for the success of the meeting? What is your accountability to contribute?

Be prepared

- Have you reviewed all the materials in advance? What are three questions you want to ask in the meeting?

- What is your initial opinion about the topic?

- What challenges do you see?

- What conversations with other participants would it be helpful to have in advance to understand the topic, or share your opinion in order to influence the outcome?

Be accountable
- What have we agreed upon?

- Are there any outstanding issues or items that need noting? Who will ensure these are followed up on? What is your role in this?

- What tasks have we agreed upon that will be completed?

- What are the deadlines for these tasks?

- What communication needs to be completed by you as a result of this meeting?

- Is there anything you are unclear about and need to clarify so you are on the right track when you leave?

Be authentic

- Review the Arc of Intense Energy at the end of this worksheet and reflect on what your automatic patterns are for meetings such as this. When stressed, how do you react? What would you like to do differently in these situations?

- What might it be uncomfortable for you to discuss as part of the meeting? Is there anything that will be contentious and others will disagree with. Are you comfortable knowing that it will be uncomfortable to speak your truth at times?

- How can you say what you need to say in the moment? Write down three points you want to get across:

- Practice noticing when your mind thinks *don't say that* for whatever reason or *that is stupid, they already know that*. Override this inner critical voice or it may stop you from being aware of your tone and speaking your truth, particularly when uncomfortable.
- Remember that this is often exactly what is needed to be put on the table in order to influence the direction the discussion needs to go.

Meeting the Owner; questions and practices for effective meetings

Review the following questions and practices to improve the effectiveness of meetings when your role is as the owner or facilitator.

Be authentic

- What is your mood as you enter into the meeting? Does this set the right tone you want? What might you have to shift in order to let go of any unhelpful energy from earlier in the day that can get in the way of the effectiveness?

- What question can you use for check-in? Do you have time for a one-sentence one, or does it need to be one word?

- What do you want to say that you might be avoiding putting on the table? How can you say what you need to while watching your tone so that it can be truly heard by participants?

HAVING EFFECTIVE MEETINGS

- Review the Arc of Intense Energy at the end of this worksheet and reflect on what your automatic patterns are for meetings such as this. When stressed, how do you react? What would you like to do differently in these situations?

- What might be uncomfortable for you to discuss as part of the meeting? Is there anything that will be contentious and others will disagree with. Are you comfortable knowing that it will be uncomfortable to speak your truth at times?

- How can you say what you need to say in the moment? Write down three points you want to get across:

- Practice noticing when your mind says *don't say that* for whatever reason or *that is stupid, they already know that* and over-ride this inner critical voice that may stop you from saying exactly what is needed in the meeting and, while being aware of your tone, speak your truth, particularly when uncomfortable.

Be inclusive

- Have you sent out the materials for the meeting, including the objective, your ask of participants, as well as, the appropriate data?

- Do you have the right participants on the meeting request?

- Do you have enough time for the discussion?

- Have you framed the objective and materials in a way that the discussion is focused on what is really needed and can be accomplished within the time you have?

- Have you left time for participants to walk to the next meeting and take a quick break before they enter into it?

- Are you sending the materials out in advance with enough time for everyone to review and reflect on them?

- What adjustments do you need to make before you send out the agenda and materials?

Be prepared

- What are the key points you want to make sure we cover?

- What points do you need to park for follow up after today?

- Do you have balanced participation? Are any more extroverted participants dominating the discussion? How will you ensure the quieter participants have an opportunity to weigh in?

- Take notes or ask a participant to take notes on what is agreed upon by when and by who.

Be clear

- Ask someone to recap what was agreed to, what tasks need to be completed, by when and by who.

- Ask the people accountable to clarify their understanding of what they will be following up on as next steps. Be careful not to only ask, *Do you agree?* But, ask them to confirm their understanding by repeating it back. Often when people say they agree, they may have a different definition of what they have agreed to and it's not discovered until they have gone down the wrong path.

- Reflect on what went well? What could have been done differently?

- Bring these learnings into your next meeting.

Arc of Intense Energy Reflection

Refer to the diagram and description of the Arc of Intense Energy on page 17. Reflect on the topic of this chapter — having effective meetings. Answer the following questions in order to understand how the arc is showing up for you:

What is your old, automatic pattern when triggered? For example, *When I am triggered by someone booking into my schedule yet another meeting when it is already full with back to back sessions, I notice I get stressed and angry and can't think straight when trying to prepare.*

What is a new behaviour, belief or attitude you would like to choose instead? For example, *When I am triggered by someone booking into my schedule yet another meeting when it is already full with back to back sessions, I notice the spike of feeling stressed moving up my spine, and my shoulders pulling up, and I call the person who booked the meeting to assess whether I need to be there or can delegate to someone else.*

Practice self-managing through the arc when you are learning about this topic. Begin by paying attention; noticing the energy or discomfort intensifying in the body. As this occurs, practice relaxing your shoulders and belly and deepen and slow your breathing.

This will allow you to feel the emotions as they arise, notice your thoughts and discern if they are aligned with your values or just old, unhelpful messages.

When you learn to discern which is true and right, you will be able to maintain your perspective and choose a response that is appropriate, and authentic, for the situation at hand.

Remember your responses to these two questions. Practice using the new behaviour, belief or attitude as your response when triggered.

After a few weeks of practicing, reflect on what you are learning and how you will adjust your thoughts and behaviours as a result.

Closing Readings:

Meetings are at the heart of an effective organization, and each meeting is an opportunity to clarify issues, set new directions, sharpen focus, create alignment, and move objectives forward.

~ Paul Axtel[52]

Meetings have morphed over the years: we gather virtually, across time zones, and often, with far less face-to-face time. Yet, one thing has not changed.

Meetings are still the prime venue to build and foster a fully inclusive culture that engages and equips people to do their very best at work.

As a leader, it's your job to make sure they do.

~ Kathryn Heath and Brenda F Wensil[53]

---

52 http://www.wiseoldsayings.com/meeting-quotes/

53 https://hbr.org/2019/09/to-build-an-inclusive-culture-start-with-inclusive-meetings

Written last as an addition to the series, this topic is foundational and can be chosen as one of the first to work through, or left to a later time once others have been worked on that are more comfortable.

This material includes new learnings about the 4-As of Authenticity, as well as, some short videos by the *Conscious Leadership Group* that will illuminate visually how the mind works.

Having authentic conversations will change your life and will change the lives of others you enter into with them.

They create more ease, deeper connections, and environments where teams can thrive, customers become raving fans, and business results improve.

Having Authentic Conversations

— Action Worksheet —

> **Topic Description:**
> I want to have Authentic Conversations!
> How can I take my mask off and be myself when it feels so vulnerable and scary?

An Authentic Person

In order to understand what authentic conversations are, it is helpful to first define authenticity. An authentic person is:

- Genuine and consistent in all parts of their life;
- Guided in a global context by a strong inner sense of the right and ethical thing to do in each moment;
- Real and honest even under stress and when triggered;
- Able to notice and let go of unhelpful patterns of thought;
- Choosing powerful life-affirming[54] actions over forceful life-destructing ones which, in doing so, supports the growth and development of the collective consciousness or the set of shared beliefs, ideas, and moral attitudes which operate as a unifying force within society;
- Having a positive ripple effect on others around them as they model authenticity for what may be the first time.

An Authentic Leader

A leader is anyone who steps up and influences others and who others choose to follow. Therefore, an authentic leader is a person who practices a way of being that is authentic in the context of influencing others.

An authentic leader serves as a role model for moral and fair behavior. A transparent approach commands esteem and confidence from others.[55]

As context for this discussion, it is helpful to understand how the mind works. This is conveyed brilliantly in two videos created and shared publicly by the *Conscious Leadership Group: Location, Location, Location*[56] also known as *Above/Below the Line* and *The Drama Triangle*[57]. Please watch them now.

---

54 Power vs. Force, David R. Hawkins.

55 MHS EQi-2.0 Assessment Report, p 6.

56 https://www.youtube.com/watch?v=fLqzYDZAqCI

57 https://www.youtube.com/watch?v=ovrVv_RICMw

Authenticity

Authenticity means having awareness of where you are located, either above or below the line, and which role you are playing in the drama triangle. It also means knowing that in every moment you have a choice. Authentic leaders use their emotional intelligence to bring themselves back above the line when it is crucial to have the right mindset and practices for approaching their conversations, decision making, and overall leadership.

An Authentic Conversation

In order to have authentic conversations you practice being authentic throughout the process, within your preparation for the conversation, during it, and even afterward when you reflect and following up.

In order to be authentic in the moment, it is helpful to become aware of the inner landscape of your thoughts, emotions and physical cues, and to use the information provided with awareness when in conversation with others.

What is an Authentic Conversation?

- What does authenticity mean?

- What are three reasons that make it important for leadership?

- How does it support interactions with others? With employees? With customers? With stakeholders? With indigenous People?

HAVING AUTHENTIC CONVERSATIONS

- Reflect on the what you are learning from each:
  Three things you learned from the video *Location, Location, Location — Above/Below the Line*:

  Three things you learned from the video *The Drama Triangle*:

  Write down three words that describe you as your authentic or best self — *Above the Line*:

  Write down one word that describes you as yourself when guided by unhelpful patterns of personality or ego — *Below the Line*:

  How will it impact your conversations if you approach it as your Authentic Self, more of the time?

The 4-As of Authenticity[58]

In order to practice awareness and then make life-affirming — *Above the Line* — choices for your actions, it is useful to practice the 4-As of Authenticity: Awakening, Awareness, Action and new Awareness.

The As for Authenticity

The cycle either starts with an awakening...
- Awakening
- Awareness
- Action
- New Awareness

The As for Authenticity

...or with initial awareness
- Awakening
- Awareness
- Action
- Awareness

Following is an example of how the 4-As for Authenticity work:

The leader of the finance department gets intimidated when presenting the budget to the executive. When he gets intimidated his stress pattern is to shut down and withdraw inward. He is not aware of this until his boss provides feedback. This creates an *awakening* or *aha* moment as he learns something new about himself that he wasn't aware of before.

Once he becomes *aware* it is occurring, he begins to notice or observe it is happening in the moment. He may realize that he is triggered by the CEO and experiences the emotion of fear. The thought that arises is that it's not safe to share his opinion and he is better to keep quiet. He saw others who shared opinions with the executive in the past and the CEO was short in her response; this has now created anxiety for the finance manager.

In the moment, he takes *action*. First, internally as he practices self-managing in order to stay present as he notices physical cues of his stress response; sweaty palms, dry throat, and tightness in his shoulders. He also notices his old pattern of getting quiet beginning to arise and he lets go of it even though it is uncomfortable. Second, he takes *action* externally as he responds with his authentic behavior which is aligned with his value of integrity and he answers the CEO's question in a respectful and confident tone.

Once the interaction is over, he has a *new awareness* of his patterns and how, in creating a new one, his confidence grows. He is positively surprised at how he was able to take a different action than he used his entire life up to this point.

---

[58] The 4-As of Authenticity are explained in more detail in my book called "Awaken Your Authentic Leadership — Lead from Inner Clarity and Purpose, Chapter 3 "How do Leaders Become Authentic", p 27.

Arc of Intense Energy Reflection

Refer to the diagram and description of the Arc of Intense Energy on page 17. Reflect on the topic of this chapter — how to have authentic conversations. Answer the following questions in order to understand how the arc is showing up for you:

What is your old, automatic pattern when triggered? For example, *When I am triggered by an employee on my team showing up and needing to talk to me right now because they are upset, I notice I get frustrated as I have too much on my plate and I keep glancing at my computer and phone as they share with me their problem.*

What is a new behaviour, belief or attitude you would like to choose instead? For example, *When I am triggered by an employee on my team showing up and needing to talk to me right now because they are upset, I notice my frustration and I override it to put down the phone, turn it off and face the person to be completely present to them.*

Practice self-managing through the arc when you are learning about this topic. Begin by paying attention; noticing the energy or discomfort intensifying in the body. As this occurs, practice relaxing your shoulders and belly and deepen and slow your breathing.

This will allow you to feel the emotions as they arise, notice your thoughts and discern if they are aligned with your values or just old, unhelpful messages.

When you learn to discern which is true and right, you will be able to maintain your perspective and choose a response that is appropriate, and authentic, for the situation at hand.

Remember your responses to these two questions. Practice using the new behaviour, belief or attitude as your response when triggered.

After a few weeks of practicing, reflect on what you are learning and how you will adjust your thoughts and behaviours as a result.

Closing Reading:

Sometimes, our instinctive reaction to being in a new situation is:
Don't be yourself.

Who else can we be? Who else would you want to be?
We don't need to be anyone else.

The greatest gift we can bring to any relationship wherever we go
is being who we are.

We may think others won't like us. We may be afraid that if we just relax and be ourselves, the other person will go away or shame us.

We may worry about what the other person will think.
But, when we relax and accept ourselves, people often feel much better being around us than when we are rigid and repressed. We're fun to be around.

If others don't appreciate us, do we really want to be around them?
Do we need to let the opinions of others control us and our behavior?

Giving ourselves permission to be who we are can have a healing influence on our relationships. The tone relaxes. We relax. The other person relaxes.....

Who we are is all we can be, all we're meant to be, and it's enough. It's fine.
Our opinion of ourselves is truly all that matters.
And we can give ourselves all the approval we want and need.

Today, I will relax and be who I am in my relationships. I will do this not in a demeaning or inappropriate way, but in a way that shows I accept myself and value who I am...[59]

---

[59] The Language of Letting Go — Daily Meditations on Codependency, Melody Beattie, p 64-65.

Bibliography

The following is a bibliography of the books and other resources that contributed to this Authentic Leadership philosophy and work.

Assessment Report — MHS EQ-i 2.0, p 6.

Bhandari, Smitha, What Does Stress do to the Body? WebMD, 2018. Reviewed by Smitha Bhandari, November 26, 2018.

Beatie, Melody, The Language of Letting Go. USA: Hazelden Foundation, 1990.

Carlson, Richard, and Joseph Bailey. Slowing down to the Speed of Life—How to create a more peaceful, simpler life from the inside out. New York: HarperCollins Books, 1997.

Effects of Stress, http://www.webmd.com/balance/stress-management/stress-management-effects-of-stress

List of Feeling Words, www.psychpage.com

George, Bill. True North — Discover your Authentic Leadership. San Francisco: Josey Bass, 2007.

George, Bill, and Peter Sims, Andrew N. McLean, and Diana Mayer. "Discovering Your Authentic Leadership." Harvard Business Review, Volume 85: No 2 (February 2007), 129 - 138.

Goleman, Daniel. Primal Leadership—Learning to Lead with Emotional Intelligence. Boston: Harvard Business School Press, 2002.

Goleman, Daniel. "What Makes a Leader?", Harvard Business Review, http://hbr.org/2004/01/what-makes-a-leader/ar/1, 1998.

Hawkins, David R. M.D., Ph.D.. Power vs Force, The Hidden Determinants of Human Behaviour. 3rd ed. Carlsbad, CA: Hay House, Inc. (Originally published in Sedona, Ariz.: Veritas Publishing), 2002.

Heminsley, Tana. Awaken Your Authentic Leadership — Lead with Inner Clarity and Purpose. Vancouver: Authentic Leadership Global, Inc. — Publishing Division.

Kornfield, Jack. A Path With Heart — A Guide through the Perils and Promises of Spiritual Life. New York: Bantam Books, 1993.

Lerner, Harriet, Ph.D. The Dance of Anger — A Woman's Guide to Changing the Patterns in Relationships. New York: Harper & Row Publishers, 2005.

Losier, Michael J. Law of Attraction — The Science of Attracting More of What you Want and Less of What you Don't. New York: Grand Central Publishing. 2009.

Movie, What the Bleep do We Know?

Movie, The Secret

Oprah Magazine. The Authentics article, March 2007.

Oriah Mountain Dreamer, The Dance — Moving to the Deep Rhythms of Your Life. New York: Harper Collins Publishers, Inc.) 2001.

Orman, Suze. The Courage to be Rich: Creating a life of material and spiritual abundance. New York:

Riverhead Books, 1999.

Professional Coaching Course, New Ventures West, http://www.newventureswest.com.

Riso, Don Richard, and Russ Hudson. The Wisdom of the Enneagram: The Complete Guide to Psychological and Spiritual Growth for the Nine Personality Types. New York: A Bantham Book, 1999.

Sams, Jami, David Carson and Angela C. Werneke. Medicine Cards: The Discovery of Power Through the Ways of Animals. New York: St. Martin's Press. 1999.

Singer, Michael A. Living from a Place of Surrender- Online Course, Session 7.

Sufi poet Rumi, as quoted by Marshall B. Rosenberg, Ph.D. in "Nonviolent Communication — A Language of Life" 2nd Edition. PuddleDancer Press: Encinatas, CA. 2005.

Tolle, Eckhart. A New Earth—Awaken to your Life's Purpose. New York: Penguin Group, 2005.

Tolle, Eckhart. A New Earth—Awakening to Your Life's Purpose—52 Inspirational Cards. New World Library Namaste Publishing.

Values (List of words), http://www.gurusoftware.com/GuruNet/Personal/Topics/Values.htm

Values (Definition) http://www.orednet.org/~jflory/205/205_val_intro.htm

Video — Location, Location, Location, by the Conscious Leadership Group.

Video — Drama Triangle, by the Conscious Leadership Group.

Wheatley, Margaret J.. Leadership and the New Science—Discovering Order in a Chaotic World. San Francisco: Berrett-Koehler Publishers, 1999.

The History of Authentic Leadership Conversations™

I've always enjoyed connecting people and building community.

The Authentic Leadership Conversation™ Dinner Series began in 2006 when I left my corporate job as an executive and became an integral leadership coach.

I wanted a way to offer clients a place where they could experience authenticity while learning about themselves, as well as, develop their ability to be authentic and built a community of support.

I was delivering retreats and I remember one new mom, who was a colleague, saying to me over tea, that she couldn't take that much time away from her family and yet she wanted to participate in a program. I asked her what her wish list was — what she wanted to talk about, how she wanted to gather with others, and how often.

The first *Authentic Leadership Conversation™ Series* was born.

I started it for women leaders initially, and we had surprisingly rich conversations over fabulous dinners in beautiful restaurants in downtown Vancouver, B.C.

For the first series, I wrote each topic before the next event, shared it in all of my nervousness with participants, and then made any final changes. I wrote a total of nine topics to begin with and added to them over the years.

I then began to offer a co-ed series for the public, as well as, by-invitation-only sessions for both senior leaders and human resource professionals. I conducted them in face-to-face groups, on conference calls, and, eventually, via skype, Webex and Zoom. I learned that once people got used to technology, the level of rich conversation was remarkable, even with others who they had never met before that session.

In 2007, one of my clients from the dinner series, asked me to come and work with his team. For four years, I facilitated lunch and dinner series with small groups of his team members. I also provided coaching for his leadership team as a group and with individuals. I shared the *Authentic You™ Personal Planning System* with them as a way to support them to develop their authentic leadership.

Since 2009 myself and my friend and colleague, Laura Mack, have been training coaches and facilitators around the world delivering the *Authentic Leadership Conversation™ Series*, as well as, several other Authentic Leadership programs for their clients.

In 2017, one of the members of the team from 2007 who was now a senior leader in the federal government called and said she had been using the Action Worksheets for all the years since we worked together initially, that we should be proud of the conversations and that it was *just what was needed for the next generation of leaders*. For a year and a half, we supported her by training facilitators and trainers of facilitators, as well as, facilitating a series of the conversations for her team.

In 2019 and 2020, we were honored to receive the *CEO Magazine Award for Management Consulting* and the results we were supporting our clients to achieve.

About the Author

Tana Heminsley is a thought-leader in the areas of authentic leadership and emotional intelligence. She is the founder of Authentic Leadership Global, Inc., a small niche firm supporting leaders to be their best and authentic selves in order to create meaningful connection and environments where their teams can thrive.

She was a facilitator of training for more than a thousand leaders through her work on *Leadership Universities* with ViRTUS.

Tana has more than thirty-five years of business and leadership experience. She worked at BC Hydro for nine years and was a member of the Executive Leadership Team from 2004 to 2006.

She has written two other books in the *Awaken Your Authentic Leadership* series on Authentic Leadership and how to be your best self as a leader.

Tana is an award-winning coach and author. She was awarded the *Vancouver Charter Chapter of International Coach Federation's 2016 Coach Impact award*. In 2019 she received the *CEO Magazine's Business Consultant Award* and was a *Book Excellence Awards Finalist* for her second book, *Awaken Your Authentic Leadership — Authenticity Journal*.

In 2018, Tana was asked to be a keynote speaker at a groundbreaking leadership and coaching conference in Beijing, China.

Tana Heminsley lives in beautiful Vancouver, British Columbia, Canada, with her husband Chris and cat Buddy.